The great Great Salt Lake

The Great Great Salt Lake

Peter G. Czerny

Brigham Young University Press

To *Victor R. Smith*
who sponsored our
family in coming to the
United States of America

Library of Congress Cataloging in Publication Data

Czerny, Peter G   1941-
The great Great Salt Lake.

Bibliography: p. 119
1. Great Salt Lake.   2. Great Salt Lake region,
Utah — Description and travel.   3. Czerny, Peter G.,
1941-   I. Title.
F832.G7C93   917.92'42   76-4080
ISBN 0-8425-1073-7

Library of Congress Catalog Card Number: 76-4080
International Standard Book Number: 0-8425-1073-7

Contents

Boulder Point at the north end of Stansbury Island is surrounded by deep water.

Acknowledgments

The completion of this book was possible only with the help of many cooperative people. My sincere thanks and grateful appreciation go to: Fred Anschutz, owner of Antelope Island, for his permission to photograph there; Henry W. Richards and associates, owners of Fremont Island; Al and Carolyn Morgan of the Bar-F Ranch near Kelton, Utah, who made my coverage of the rugged northwest areas of the lake most pleasurable through their gracious hospitality; Richard and Lori Nicholas and other residents of East Promontory, who initiated me into this inaccessible area; ranchers and farmers and their employees who gave me permission to photograph on their properties; employees of the Southern Pacific Transportation Company and the lake area; Mr. Barry B. Combs of the Public Relations Department of the Union Pacific Railroad Company; and Susan E. Williams of the Oakland Museum.

I would also like to thank officials and employees of Hill Air Force Base; employees of the Historian's Office of The Church of Jesus Christ of Latter-day Saints, of the Utah State Historical Society, of the Rare Collection Department at Marriott Library, University of Utah, and of firms and companies established in the lake areas who so willingly cooperated in this project.

David E. Miller, chairman of the Utah Committee on Geographic Names, and committee members Jay Haymond, Jahn VanCott, Kent Malan, Earl Olsen, Theron Luke, and Wendy Hassibe were also helpful.

Many other individuals helped in one way or another to complete this book: Bennie Hastings, John Goodwin, Jim Ried and the late Dale Helfer — my helicopter pilots — whose expert flying and maneuvering made many of the pictures possible; Norman Ricks, who flew me over the lake several times; John Silver and his family at Silver Sands Marina; members of the Great Salt Lake Yacht Club; Elvin Beaumont and his swamp boat; Les Hunt, caretaker of the Antelope Island ranch; Reed Smoot, Mark Eubank, Jim Dearden, Jim Ward, Roy Birrell, Grant Fredrickson, Lionel Brown, Mary Louise Seamons, and Jerry Ewell of Salt Lake Sailboats, all of whom helped in various ways.

A special thanks goes to Spencer G. Lewis and Gerald Hatch who backed me up with their cameras during the helicopter flights, taking many pictures I would not have obtained otherwise. Mr. Lewis accompanied me on several subsequent helicopter flights and contributed some free-lance work that has added variety and interest to this work.

I am grateful to Derrell J. Stoddard and his father Earl S. Stoddard for their information about the Fremont Island Indians and for allowing me to photograph their artifact collection.

For the continuing encouragement that gave me the motivation to complete this book I give credit to my parents and family members and to Hilde P. Mueller.

A final thanks goes to Jean R. Paulson for help in organizing and compiling the manuscript, and to Louise Hanson, editor, and McRay Magleby, designer, at Brigham Young University Press for smoothing the whole into the finished product.

Introduction

Great Salt Lake, the mineral-rich inland sea whose heavy waters are six times saltier than the oceans, has been the topic of debate and speculation since it was discovered by mountain men. But in all their conjecture about the lake's mysteries, people have somehow forgotten to simply look at it and enjoy it.

For my fellow Utahns, this book will show a lake they hardly know. For others, it will be an armchair exploration of a strange body of water. For everyone, it will present advice on how to enjoy the lake, such as coping with the salty water and the harmless brine shrimp. It will also be a guide to out-of-the-way areas in and around the lake.

It is not my intention to write a complete history of the lake, since that has been done in books, pamphlets, and other studies. Despite the number of such studies in print, however, there is not a single photo-book. It is this gap I hope to fill.

My fascination with the lake is rooted in my childhood in Germany. As a boy, I was spellbound when someone told me about a lake where you could float and not have to know how to swim. The maps showed me a railroad trestle crossing the lake, and when my family emigrated from Germany to the United States, the first thing I wanted to do was to cross the Great Salt Lake on that trestle.

When we settled in Clearfield, I first saw the lake, a wide band of quicksilver glistening twenty miles to the west. Intrigued, I walked toward it, but soon realizing the distance was deceiving, I turned back.

At North Davis Junior High School, during my last class period I could see the lake through the windows, sparkling in the distance as it cast its spell of attraction on me. When we moved to West Point, much closer to the lake, I spent countless hours on top of the silo at the Lee Thurgood farm looking west to the lake. I wondered about the mountains on the other side and about climbing to the top of Antelope Island. I would have given anything to stand near the airway beacon on that island as it flashed its direction-giving light. I explored the marshy shores near West Point, but the lake was always a little farther away.

Later we moved to Salt Lake City, and it was here that I finally met the lake. Frequent family outings to Black Rock Beach and nearby areas increased the enchantment I felt from this fascinating body of brine. The exhilarat-ing water, the hardy breeze with its unusual salty tang, the blazing sunsets confirmed what I had always felt: Great Salt Lake was indeed great.

While I was attending the University of Utah in Salt Lake City, the lake became a friend. If I was troubled, if I needed to overcome feelings of *fernweh* (the desire to "get away from it all"), Great Salt Lake was the cure. The lake would perk me up, renew my spirit, rejuvenate my soul.

Once, at Sand Pebble Beach, I wrote a poem, "The Lake as a Friend," crystallizing some of my thoughts about the lake. Although it does not translate into English in poetic form, the last two stanzas, appended here, reflect my feelings.

The deepest of my sorrows,
My heaviest heartaches
I could quietly lament here;
The lake would listen.

Once I tasted its water
And would never have imagined
It tasted bitter, like tears;
The lake had wept with me.

No one thing attracts me to the lake; it has many allurements. Like the evergreen tree that never loses its greenery, the lake is perennially vital; it never freezes, and on a sunny winter day you can stand on its shore and catch a glimpse of far-off summer.

Great Salt Lake has been called an extension of the desert, yet some of the most beautiful views in a picturesque country can be found in and around it. Perhaps its greatest attraction is that it is virtually unchanged by civilization. Here one can touch history, walk where primitive Indians walked, follow the steps of early explorers and pioneers, see nature as it was seen hundreds of years ago. Here one can say, in truth, "This is the way it was."

Here, then, is a photographic look at a lake that has witnessed prodigious engineering feats, high adventure, and bizarre events. It has been a continuous adventure for me to explore it all and to photograph it. I have rescued people and have been rescued; have crash-landed in a small plane after a photo flight; have fallen down a steep slope onto rocks; have fought a bad storm in a swamp boat only to have a high wave short out the power. But "oh, the thrill of it all!" (John S. Hart.)

In his book *The Great Salt Lake*, the late Dale L. Morgan described the lake as "intolerant of men and reluctant in submission to their uses." The water defends itself with its own shallows from the incursions of man. Yet, those very shallows, graduating downward from the usable beaches, have made the lake a delight for bathers from all over the world who have floated in its buoyant waters.

The other problems? They are challenges to be met with careful preparation and common sense.

Caution is called for when you explore the remote and uninhabited west sides of the lake where ancient Lake Bonneville left its brackish residue. There, patches of salt grass, greasewood, gray-green sage, and splotches of juniper decline into a vast plain of shimmering nothingness — the Salt Flats. Go prepared when you venture into this grim and forbidding land. I have spent many days in the western areas, never once seeing another human. Take plenty of gasoline, water, food, and protective gear. I always carry an extra tire, a pump, a tire repair kit, a heavy-duty jack, a two-ton winch, an ax, a heavy crowbar and tools, extra fuses, a flashlight, matches, and an extra fan belt.

I have been doubly cautious when I have gone alone — a venture I do not recommend. In the Hogup-Terrace mountains, while visiting the Hogup Indian cave, I was more than fifty miles from the nearest ranch in Kelton, which didn't even have a telephone.

As for the lake itself, by using foresight and prudence, the bather will find that it is a place for enjoyment where he can float in total relaxation while absorbing an atmosphere of haunting loveliness.

My biggest breakthrough to enjoying the lake came through my desire to swim in places where there were no facilities for showering off the salt water. Fresh-water showers are necessary since, on exposure to air and sunlight, the salt water crystallizes on the skin and on small body hairs. How could I get along without such a shower? My first experiment — just letting it happen — was a painful lesson. My clothing became sandpaper, every move caused an irritating pain, and it was days before my roughed-up skin returned to normal.

Next I tried oily lotions and creams to repel the water, but these only left a hard-to-remove goo on my skin. Some weeks later, still attempting to solve the problem, I got wet, walked along the beach, and found that the bothersome crystals started to form. Back in the water again, the crystals dissolved.

Then, while floating, the breakthrough idea hit me — the Q2 Method, which stands for quick-dry and two towels. Here is the way it works: When you are completely wet and all crystals are dissolved, step out of the water quickly and soak off all the water with the first towel, completing the job with the second. Do a thorough drying job, and the water will be removed before the salt can crystallize. Then dry the towels in the sun, shake them out, and they're ready for the next swim.

This method has worked so well for me during the past few years that I don't take a shower even when one is available. The skin has a tingling aliveness after a salt water dry-off. By using the Q2 Method one can enjoy superior swimming areas other than those in the commercialized southeast, to be described in later chapters.

Although diving has been discouraged because the salt water surface is harder than fresh water, and water can get in the bather's eyes when he surfaces, diving from relatively low levels is feasible. I have seen people jump off boats headfirst into the wake with no ill effects. To keep salt water out of his eyes, a bather need only flick his fingers across his closed eyes upon surfacing. Another time-tested method is to suck the forefinger clean of salt water then wash salt from the eyes with saliva.

Small children should simply not be allowed in the water; they are not able to cope with the effects of salt in the eyes or with the choking in the event they swallow a mouthful of water.

One secret of enjoying out-of-the-way places is to carry a plentiful supply of insect repellent. The most potent and best working insect repellents are usually in a rub-on form and have about 40 percent or more of the active ingredient N,N-Diethyl-meta-toluamide. Rub it into your skin and along the edges of your socks and cuffs. You may need to reapply it after a swim.

By wearing lightweight goggles in the water you can prevent burning eyes, making sure to keep the goggles wet to prevent their caking with salt. To guard against swallowing a salty wave, keep your mouth closed, and be cautious when the wind stirs up waves. It is most enjoyable to float when the wind stirs the cumbrous water,

Early morning calm and light transform the Silversands Marina into a peaceful haven.

lulling the floater with a bobbing roller-coaster motion — a relaxing antidote to tension and worry.

It is wise to wear sneakers around beach areas and in the water to prevent skin punctures from sharp items left by man and from salt crystals precipitated on the beach when the lake is low and the salt content high.

When the lake is calm, there is a way to float that affords complete relaxation. Let your limbs dangle where they will as you relax, then allow your head to sink slowly back, allowing your hair to get wet. As your head sinks farther back, the water will reach about to your eyes, but at that point the heavy salt water will support your head, and you can float, using no muscles, carried completely by the water. This experience is so pleasant — like lying in clouds — that I have lain this way for hours, never moving a muscle.

Brine flies and brine shrimp, minor annoyances for the bather, are harmless enough. The shrimp are so small that they can't be felt on the skin, and if a few remain after the bather leaves the water, they disappear in the drying process. The flies, thoroughly lazy, don't sting or bite, but if disturbed will fly up, landing a few feet away to bask again in the heat. On the west side and on the islands, gnats are abundant, but repellent will keep them at bay. In early spring, when winter gray turns green, there is a period when one can visit any area of the lake and find no insects. Although it is too cold for swimming, I always go to the lake at this time, for it is at its best.

Sailing in the northern half of the lake is not recommended. First, access is next to impossible, and second, the water has reached the saturation point of salt, which forms thick layers of salt crystals on the bottom of the lake. These layers can rip into a hull, causing heavy damage.

But in other parts of the lake sailing is popular, since the lake doesn't freeze in the winter and offers a year-around surface for sailing and racing. In the summertime the lake breeze is refreshing, and the "world's saltiest sailors" put up with the inconvenience of having the spray crystallize on deck and clothing. At the docks, fresh water is available for hosing off.

Sudden storms and lack of experience on the part of boatmen are the two most dangerous elements in boating and sailing on the Great Salt Lake. Strong currents and high winds can take a boat into shallow areas or smash it on a rocky beach. Large sailboats are made to withstand heavy winds, but even in these the occupants can get seasick. Salt-water waves pack almost twice the punch of an equivalent fresh-water wave. Some sailors compare a three-foot chop against a boat in Great Salt Lake with the power of a five-foot chop of fresh water.

Years ago, people refrained from taking their motorboats onto the lake because of the corrosiveness of the salt water, but today, because of the corrosion-proof metals with which motors are made, this is no longer a concern.

In his exploration of the lake and its surroundings, a visitor should remember that construction or private ownership can close or change roads and areas. Private properties should be respected. Since many of the roads are unimproved, the traveler is advised to exercise caution when using them. Crossing the Great Salt Lake Desert on these primitive roads can be dangerous. One sudden thunderstorm and the traveler is surrounded by impassible mud flats, particularly at the uninhabited west and northerly sides of the lake.

The map included in this book will serve two purposes: as a guide to the areas discussed and as a reference to areas where many of the photographs were taken. When I started collecting pictures of the lake and its environs, I found that many geological features were yet unnamed, making it difficult for sailors and land rovers to rendezvous near to or to talk about certain areas. For this reason I obtained permission from the Utah Committee on Geographic Names and the U.S. Board of Geographic Names to provide designations for those unnamed areas. Consequently, no longer is it necessary to talk about "the first bay on the east side of Stansbury Island"; now it can be called Sandy Beach Bay. Other points of interest, such as interesting rocks and prominent features, are also on the map.

Current and future plans for the development of recreational facilities on the Great Salt Lake are extensive. A seasonal causeway to the north shore of Antelope Island has been constructed, and at the self-recreational park on the island a visitor's center has been planned. Furthermore, with the expected acquisition of land on the south shore of the lake at Silver Sands Beach, officials of the Utah State Parks and Recreation Department plan to expand the marina there and to add to the existing water and beach sports. A general up-

At the Silversands Marina a handful of sailors are anxious to launch before night falls.

grading of the facilities on the lake will attract not only natives of Utah but also tourists from all over the nation. Already one of the marvels of the world, Great Salt Lake is destined to become a mecca for travelers who seek both beauty and recreation.

A wealth of places to go and things to see await the visitor to the Great Salt Lake. Chapters four through thirteen, along with the map, guide the reader on a full-circle tour around the lake — beginning at its southeast end.

Facts about the Lake

America's Dead Sea, the largest body of water in the Western United States, has, because of the unusual makeup of its water, been the subject of numerous books and articles. The strangeness and the mysterious qualities of the lake and its adjacent areas are threads that run through these accounts, whether written by scholars or by writers for the popular market.

Thanks to scientific studies, some of which are encapsulated in a review of United States Senate hearings held in Ogden and Salt Lake City in 1960, as well as to other accounts, you don't have to taste the lake's brine to know that it is about one-fourth salt. The facts listed in this and subsequent chapters are substantiated in the volumes listed in the bibliography at the back of this book, including accounts of early explorations and the comprehensive survey made by Howard Stansbury and his party in 1850.

One built-in phenomenon that could keep the lake from disappearing — as one scientist years ago predicted it would — is that the more the lake shrinks and the saltier it becomes, the lower the evaporation rate is. Even normally the water evaporates slowly, about 75 to 80 percent of the rate of fresh water evaporation.

The sun, always pulling at the lake with its evaporative powers, plays a strange role in the life of the lake. Two years after sun spot activity is lowest, according to Leonard Zimmerman, the lake usually reaches the highest point of a rising cycle.

In some cycles the inflow of fresh water is not equal to the constant pull of evaporation, and the lake shrinks. The three principal affluents of the lake — the Bear, Weber, and Jordan rivers — supply only 43 percent of the inflow needed to offset evaporation. The rest is supplied by minor runoff, underground springs, and rainfall. The Bear, the largest river in North America that doesn't reach the ocean, pours 1.2 million acre feet of water annually into the Great Salt Lake.

A force more powerful than the river's flow is the occasional wind that whips the ponderous water into waves that have been known to push rocks weighing up to one-half ton onto the railroad dams. Another force, settling, keeps the dike builders busy. Some dikes have been built to an overall height of seventy-two feet to offset their sinking into the lake bottom.

In view of the riches stored in the lake, it is ironic that in 1873 a study was made to see if the lake could be drained into Nevada to get rid of it once and for all. It was later determined that there are about 120 million tons of potash and 4½ billion tons of salt suspended in the water. The brine shrimp were harvested later and sold for fish food, and tourism added uncounted millions to Utah's treasury.

Visitors who get a mouthful of the brine can take some solace in the fact that the lake contains enough salt to supply the nation's needs for the next 200 to 240 years. The salt, and the other chemicals suspended in the water, are valued at thirty-two times more than the assessed value of the entire state of Utah as of 1960.

As time is measured geologically, that salt is new to the area. Anciently, a fresh water lake nearly as large as Lake Michigan covered much of northern Utah and contiguous areas in Idaho and Nevada. About 145 miles wide and 345 miles long, the lake went through three major levels, the first of which, the Bonneville, gave the lake a depth of more than one thousand feet. When it reached the top of Red Rock Pass in northern Cache Valley, it overflowed into the Snake River, a tributary of the Columbia. As the pass was worn down by the massive overflow, the lake dropped dramatically about 375 feet. Here, at the Provo level, the lake stabilized and remained for the longest of the three periods. Subsequent climate changes increased evaporation, and the lake shrank to its third, the Stansbury, level. After a period of rising and falling it declined to the present fluctuating level of the Great Salt Lake.

Terraces gouged into the mountain sides by the abrasive waves show many intermediate levels. As the fresh water evaporated, minerals which had been widely dispersed became concentrated. Lacking natural outlets, the lake hoarded the mineral deposits until it built up to its present salty state.

Since man has kept records of these level changes, a level difference of some twenty feet has been observed, the highest 4,211 feet above sea level in the mid-1870s, and the lowest 4,191, in the mid-1960s.

The lake level is recorded by the location of its surface in relationship to sea level. Thus, if the lake's level is at 4,200 feet, it doesn't mean the lake is 4,200 feet deep, but that its surface is at 4,200 feet above sea level, at which point the lake is only about thirty-four feet deep. All calculations regarding the lake's rising or falling can be made with these base figures. At a maximum depth of twenty-nine feet, the lake level is 4,195 feet above sea level; at the 4,203-foot lake level, it is thirty-seven feet at its deepest.

Since the bottom is flat, with little sloping, a drop of a foot or two in the level exposes miles of lake bottom, even surrounding the islands. The huge mud flats reduce the picturesque quality of the lake. But at the 4,200-foot level most islands lose their sandbanks; the bays fill with water, and only the western shores, flattest of all, keep their mud flats, rising gently to a white, salt-encrusted beach.

Salinity of the water varies with the changes in the level. Heavy spring runoffs dilute the salt content; dry seasons shrink the lake and increase the salt content. The northern half, cut off by a railroad dam, gets little fresh water, and here salinity is highest, averaging from 20 to 25 percent.

With that kind of salinity, life in the water is limited. Although dead fish are seen at times, these are carried in, already dead, by the streams. One visible organism thriving in the lake is the tiny brine shrimp — pinkish-transparent and measuring no longer than ½ inch. Millions exist in the water. Other living organisms in the brine are a blue-green algae (prevalent in the southern half of the lake and food for the shrimp), some protozoans, a few bugs, and flies. Brine flies often blacken the beaches as they bask in the sun, and their pupal shells wash to the shore, sometimes fouling water, beach, and air. The red algae is so concentrated in the stronger brine at the north that the water has a red tint.

If there isn't much variety of life in the water, however, there is an abundance of life on and around it. Bird refuges have been established along the eastern shores where inflowing fresh water has created vast marshes. Other life on some islands and the surrounding areas include coyotes, wild rabbits, small rodents, and rattlesnakes. I've seen deer in the northern areas and on Antelope Island, which is also home for a herd of buffalo.

Mineral extraction is big business, and several companies extract salt, using solar evaporation to reclaim it. Water is pumped into ponds, evaporated by the sun, and the process repeated to build a salt layer. The salt is then scooped up, processed, and sold. A few firms extract magnesium and other metallic elements and chemicals. Elements suspended in the water include sulfate, magnesium, potassium, calcium, and traces of others, along with chlorine and sodium.

The deepest part of the lake, thirty-four feet when the surface is at 4,200 feet above sea level, is along the center section of the railroad trestle. Because of the buoyancy, a diver descending to thirty-four feet would have to rig himself with weights and pressure gear as if diving several hundred feet into the ocean. On calm days the heavy water lies still, but when whipped up by winds it packs a vigorous wallop. Sailors are aware of this and on stormy days remain ashore, since the wind and waves can knock a vessel about, and salt spray in the eyes can hinder a sailor from rigging and adjusting sails. Many sailboats carry a motor for quick trips back to the dock in case of storms.

Most of the islands and the best scenery are south of the railroad dam. Gunnison Island, which might be set aside as a refuge to protect the large pelican colony, is the only island of note on the north side of the lake.

Those who sail the lake regularly report unusual experiences. At times, the wind-whipped water is like the ocean in a storm; minutes later the surface can be a mirror, with hardly a ripple. It is during these calm times, especially at night, that the lake becomes eerie. Lights on the horizon play tricks.

Sound carries unpredictably over the waters. Several boaters have reported chilling experiences. As they floated in calm waters far out on the lake, the silence was shattered by the insane yammering of coyotes, their short-syllable barks ringing and counter-ringing in a rising crescendo of discord as if the animals were only a few feet away. Yet the nearest land was miles distant.

Twilight hours take on a mystic aspect when objects along the shore shroud themselves in the dying light. Sometimes it is difficult to distinguish where water and sky meet, and if there is no breeze to carry sounds, one is surrounded by an overpowering silence.

The Great Salt Lake is an antinomy. One hour you enjoy a delightful boating experience; the next, you fear for your life as huge waves wash into the vessel. One minute you thrill as you float as if on clouds; the next, you struggle to swim to the shore. On one beach you frolic in clean white sand; on another, you sink knee-deep in black, stinking mud. One year all the bays are filled with water; another, the islands are surrounded

A seagull floats motionless in the air as an oncoming breeze gives it lift. It is hovering above its nest.

by miles of crusty, salty mud flats. One day the water sparkles like a sapphire; the next day it is murky and dark. On a single day I have seen it change from clear to dark, from blue to green and to all shades between. The color varies with the season, the weather, and the depth of water, and in the early spring you can view the lake at a prismatic level unmatched during other seasons.

To enjoy the lake the visitor must realize that there are extremes, that no one can foretell them, and that he should accept the lake as it is.

GARFIELD BEACH
OR SAVAGE PL

Pictures of the Past

Early adventurers explored the lake happily and otherwise. One of the most celebrated was Baron La Hontan, lord-lieutenant of Placentia, Newfoundland, who "explored" the lake second-handedly — through Indians' stories about it. It was through him that the outside world received its first inkling that there was a salt water lake in North America. He explored parts of the continent in 1689 and published some of his accounts in 1735.

The first part of his account, although the rivers and areas have unfamiliar names, are clearly about the Mississippi and Missouri rivers, adjacent areas, and Indian tribes. Later, the story becomes confused, for part of his descriptions are hearsay, a recounting of what Indians had observed. It is in this section that he mentions a salt lake, beside which were many Indian settlements. Unfortunately, his vivid description, along with a map including a great river flowing into the lake and another great river flowing out of it all the way to the Pacific Ocean, originated much mystery and confusion about the lake.

Historic markers throughout the state, which today's explorers can see (One such marker is at the [Utah] County Building in Provo), attest to the first concrete knowledge of the Great Salt Lake. These markers tell of a Spanish expedition to the interior basin by Father Dominguez and Father Escalante in a search for a feasible route to California. Setting out from Santa Fe July 29, 1776, they entered Utah Valley September 23 through Spanish Fork Canyon and met and befriended Indians from whom they learned of a salt lake to the north connected to the fresh water (Utah) lake by a river. In his diary Escalante writes:

The other lake with which this one communicates, according to what they told us, covers many leagues, and its waters are noxious and extremely salty, for the Timpanois assure us that a person who moistens any part of his body with the water of the lake immediately feels much itching in the part that is wet. Round about it, they told us, live a numerous and peaceful nation called Puaguampe, which in our ordinary speech means "Witch Doctors" and who speak the Cumanche language. Their food consists of herbs. They drink from several fountains or springs of good water which are around the lake, and they have houses of grass and earth (the earth being used for the roofs). They are not

enemies of the Lagunas, according to what they intimated, but since a certain occasion when [the Puaguampes] approached and killed one of their men they do not consider them as neutral as formerly.

This is the first authentic description of the lake and its environs, even though the explorers did not travel north to see it. Interestingly, they were not told that a person doesn't sink in the water; possibly the skins of the Indians smarted so in the brine that they never went deep enough to float. Don Bernardo de Miera, whose fame as a mappist persists today, mapped the party's travels, showing Great Salt Lake to the north of Utah Lake, with a river flowing out of it toward California. He connected the two lakes, calling them by one name, and added his considerable prestige to the legend of the great river running westward to the ocean.

Jim Bridger is generally credited with being the first white man to see the Great Salt Lake, but he thought it was the Pacific Ocean. That was in 1824. Bridger's misconception was dispelled in 1826 when trapper James Clyman and three companions circled the lake in a bull boat and found it had no western outlet.

Six years later, in 1832, Captain Bonneville, on leave from the army, trapped and explored in the west, and a party of his men, en route to California, explored the lake and gave a good description. Other facts known today came to light as travel through the Great Basin increased. One of Bonneville's party, Zenas Leonard, writing about this exploration in 1839, was probably the first to report that the lake, shrinking in the hot months, leaves salt deposits on the shores.

Through a report by James Clyman, who saw the lake again in 1846, we learn that the shrinking was cyclical over a period of years. He reported that the lake had lost half its size in the twenty years since he first saw it.

Three years earlier than this, in 1842, John C. Fremont visited the island now named for him, in an India-rubber boat, calling it "Disappointment Island." He had expected to find a tropical paradise.

The name, the Great Salt Lake, seems to have come by way of mouth since the earliest references to the lake were simply that of a salt lake. When it was finally seen and circled, the trappers and explorers were awed by its size. It was probably just a natural addition to refer to it as the "great" salt lake.

A new era for the lake began in 1847 when Brigham

Beck's Hot Springs near the Jordan River delta used natural thermal waters to lure bathers.

Young and his first parties of Mormon pioneers arrived to make the first permanent settlement near its shores. The Mormons found enjoyment bathing in the lake and in nearby hot and cold springs. From these pioneers we have the first account that a person floats corklike on the water.

Two years later enough interest had generated about the lake that the U.S. Army's Corps of Topographical Engineers sent a surveying expedition from Washington, D.C. Led by Captain Howard Stansbury, assisted by Lieutenant J. W. Gunnison, the party arrived in Salt Lake City August 28, 1849. Stansbury decided to circle the lake and the western desert before winter and to start surveying in the spring.

Running out of water on the west side, the party forcemarched to Pilot Peak to replenish the supply. The desert's toll was the lives of three mules. Returning, the men saw the abandoned wagons, skeletons of animals, and other effects of earlier desert crossers. In his *Exploration and Survey of the Great Salt Lake Valley* Stansbury writes:

During the night, we passed five wagons and one cart, which had stuck fast in the mud, and been necessarily left by their owners, who, from appearances, had abandoned every thing, fearful of perishing themselves in this inhospitable desert. Great quantities of excellent clothing, tool-chests, trunks, scientific books, and, in fact, almost every thing, both useless and necessary on a journey of this kind, had been here left strewn over the plain. Many articles had not even been removed from the wagons. The carcasses of several oxen lying about on the ground satisfactorily explained the whole matter. In attempting to cross the plain, the animals had died from exhaustion and want of water, and the wagons and their contents had of course to be abandoned.

Stansbury had started this trip with five men and sixteen mules on October 19. They returned, exhausted, on November 7. Through this trip they became aware that the survey would be exhausting labor and a battle to find fresh water.

Starting the actual survey on April 2, 1850, Stansbury set up triangulation stations on all islands and a few nearby mountains in order to verify his survey with a series of triangles. Hardships became routine. They were marooned on a mud flat in a snowstorm, were beset by constant worry over the water supply, and had

Rare, panoramic view of the Garfield resort and Garfield's Landing.

The Garfield pavilion — a popular pre-Saltair resort.

to drag their boat, The Salicornia (Sally) and a skiff over miles of inch-deep water. Several times they were hopelessly stuck until a change in the wind pushed water their way, giving some lift to their boat. The worst plague was gnats. As they crossed the marshy flats, all hands occupied dragging the boat, the black hordes swarmed onto them. The only reprieve was when they were in deeper water.

Some of the survey party left to seek gold in California, but others replaced them and the work pushed through to completion. The party left the lake on July 16, 1850. Stansbury's report is fascinating. In it he also describes a route to Fort Hall, proposes a new route for immigrants, describes a survey of Utah Lake, and writes interestingly of his travels to and from Utah.

Meanwhile, the lake gained in popularity. At first only a few made the trip from the city to Black Rock with horse and buggy, but with the arrival of the Utah Central Railroad, linking Salt Lake City and Ogden, this changed. The railroad line came nearest to the lake at Farmington, and near here the Lake Side Resort opened in 1870.

Later, steamboat service was added, and the *City of*

Black Rock and pier, with Antelope Island in the distance.

Private home near Black Rock.

popularity dwindled as that of Garfield increased. The Garfield resort is well described in Dale L. Morgan's book, *The Great Salt Lake:*

This new resort, the proprietors boasted, was distinguished by a magnificent pavilion, 165 by 65 feet, built over the water 400 feet from shore, and approached by a covered pier over 300 feet in length. The whole was surmounted by an observation tower overlooking the lake on all sides, and in this pavilion, every afternoon during the season, a grand concert was to be given by "a first-class orchestra of talented soloists." There were elegant dressing rooms, a handsome station building, a restaurant and lunchstand with a distinguished bill of fare, and a saloon where the choicest brands of liquors and cigars would be dispensed by polite attaches. It was also to be borne in mind that Garfield Beach was the only resort on the entire lake shore having a clean, sandy beach, free from mud, rocks and offensive vegtable matter.

The success of Garfield bred competition. In 1893, the pavilion at Saltair was completed, and the famous Saltair resort was born. It was grander than any of the

Corinne made runs between Corinne and the south end of the lake at Lake Point. In 1872, Lake Side became home port for the steamer, and Lake Point, at the south end of the lake, became a resort, for a traveler could catch the steamer here as well.

Another resort was established at Black Rock after the Utah Western Railroad built a line to that point, and the *City of Corinne*, renamed the *General Garfield*, made its home base at Lake Point, near Black Rock, in order to cash in on the business at the popular south end.

The owner of the steamboat finally decided to go into the resort business; so he moved his craft to Garfield's Landing, where it was permanently docked. Later a resort was built around it. This was called Garfield Beach.

Lake Side was losing status, and the Denver and Rio Grande Western Railroad Company, laying a track to Ogden in 1886, built a resort north of Lake Side and west of Syracuse, naming it Lake Park. Although frequented by tens of thousands of visitors, this beach was not so attractive as those on the southern end, and its

The private home now a ruin (ca. 1936).

The General Garfield and sightseers await launching.

others and boasted a train transporting passengers into the resort, which was supported on pillars thrusting out of the water. The spectacular dome was patterned after the Mormon Tabernacle on Temple Square. Since there was no beach, bathers entered the water from steps.

Saltair soon outdrew the Garfield crowds, but Garfield remained in competition until it burned down in 1904. That left Saltair as the reigning resort. Music from famous bands echoed over the waters, tourists from all parts of the world made it a destination, drawn not only by the bathing but by the later-built amusement park and its hair-raising, death-defying roller coaster ride — the main attraction.

Unfortunately, the bubble of glory deflated as steadily as the Great Salt Lake shrank. First, people had to walk to the water just beyond the pavilion, then farther and farther until the short walk became a long hike. Saltair was doomed. As it struggled for survival, the competition looked farther south. A resort was built on Black Rock Beach in 1933 and another, Sunset Beach, on Fritch Island in 1934.

Although these new resorts lacked the magnificence of Saltair, they did have water, a beach, a good auto-mobile road, and even a rock-lined harbor as the results of efforts by the Great Salt Lake Yacht Club and Salt Lake County. Inadequate, and too small for the seventy-five to 100 sailboats docked there, it nevertheless permitted boating, heretofore neglected because of the water's inaccessibility. The shallow nature of all the beaches made launching a cumbersome operation until the harbor was dredged.

For a few years the resort situation remained stable. Saltair was hanging on, rebuilding after fires, until the war years slowed everything down.

During the late 1940s, as the lake rose a little, the resort business picked up, but starting in the early 1950s the lake began a ten-year period of decline that brought even Black Rock and Sunset Beach to their knees. Finally, Saltair, inoperative and decaying, burned. Black Rock was next to fall, closing in the early 1960s when the water had withdrawn too far from the resort. Its handsome fresh water pool soon filling with sand, the resort stood for several years, abandoned, until the hand of an arsonist put it out of its misery. I remember that night vividly. I had driven to the lake, little dreaming that I would see the resort ablaze. From afar, I stood in silence, tears rolling down my cheeks. Black Rock Resort was gone.

A few years later I noticed that Sunset Beach Resort had vanished from Fritch Island.

Only one latecomer survived. Started in 1964 on the foundation of the burned-out County Boat Harbor, Silver Sands Beach had stayed alive. Attractions included a beach contrived of hauled-in sand, rides on an amphibious vehicle, *The Seamonster*, and a fifty-seven foot catamaran yacht, *The Islander*, added in 1970. The yacht offered sightseeing and a dinner cruise. Silver Sands was now the only place where the visitor could get information about the lake or see those famous sunsets from the beach.

But the lake began to rise. Soon the beaches at Silver Sands disappeared beneath the water, and other beaches lost their mud flats. The higher lake level encouraged more boating, especially sailing, and the Silver Sands people turned their attention to providing docks. Since the beach was gone, the name was changed to Silver Sands Marina. Bathers now had to fend for themselves on adjacent unimproved beaches; all commercial efforts centered on the harbor.

A sight-seeing steamer lies motionless near the shore of the lake, reflected in mirror-calm water.

Early view of the grand Saltair Pavilion. Fires resulted in subsequent rebuilding and changes in appearance.

The world-famous dance hall in the Saltair pavilion.

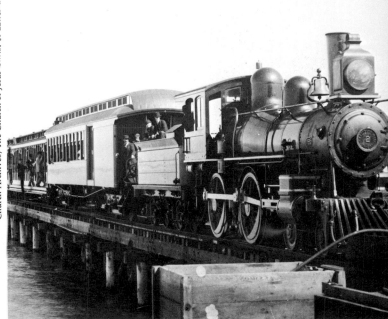

The Saltair Special steamed into the resort on a trestle.

Boat owners had it better. More than 200 berths had been created, and new life sparkled on the lake. Boat parties, races, regattas, and the commotion of a busy harbor gave the area an oceanic flair. Buying out private interests, the state took over the entire southeast shore and made plans to enlarge the harbor, improve the beaches, establish concessions, build parking lots, and make the area available to the public.

The State Park Commission administers the area, along with the Great Salt Lake State Park at Antelope Island, which had been closed for several years since the access road was washed out. The high lake level dictates the need to develop the beaches — perhaps with another Saltair — so that the lake can be utilized while it is high.

In addition to the fascinating lives of the resorts, many other items of historic interest are connected with the lake. Only twelve miles from its shores one of the greatest feats of all time was completed when, on May 10, 1869, the last spike — a golden one — was driven at Promontory, Utah, celebrating the construction of a railroad spanning the North American continent. Here the Central Pacific Railroad from the West joined the Union Pacific Railroad from the East. The days of extreme hardships encountered in driving wagon trains across plains and mountains were over. A journey that had required months of time and back-breaking labor could now be accomplished in four days. It is hard to find an event in American history, save the day of independence itself, that held such significance and benefit for every individual.

Twenty-three miles westward at Monument Point the tracks of the Central Pacific came nearest the lake. Here you could almost throw a stone from the train to the water. Passengers could see the lake for hours as they emerged from Weber Canyon, then passed through Ogden and Corinne, climbed the Promontory Summit, and rounded Spring Bay toward Kelton.

In 1903 the circuitous route was straightened by a pile-trestle costing $8.5 million, extending directly west from Ogden over the lake, saving time and mileage. Piles up to 150 feet long were driven into the lakebed, making it possible to go to sea by rail, a novelty attracting many tourists. A station house, Midlake, built on pillars, became the destination for passengers enjoying the thrilling ride over the lake.

Construction of the Lucin Cutoff in 1903.

Salt crystals on the piles of the Lucin Cutoff.

Heading west to San Francisco, a passenger train crosses the Great Salt Lake on the Lucin Cutoff trestle.

The Lake Park resort near Syracuse gears up for a Fourth-of-July celebration.

The Lake Park resort as seen from the water's edge.

A more recent view of Saltair which, by this time, had added an amusement park.

24

The original Great Salt Lake Boat Harbor, about 1950.

The Kate Conner, *early freighter on the Great Salt Lake, sits mired on the banks of the Bear River, near Corinne.*

One of the two tugboats that dredged the south end of the Great Salt Lake for a crashed DC 3 (1936).

View of the Black Rock resort and beach (ca. late 1930s).

After five months' burial in the Great Salt Lake, the crashed DC 3 is lifted out of its briny grave.

Fire razed sections of the trestle at times; so the Southern Pacific Railroad Company built an earth-fill dam. But this, too, needs constant attention, since the waves are damaging. Rising water in the past two years even threatened to wipe out the dam, but the S.P. was foresighted enough to keep the old trestle in repair, and on stormy days the trains cross over it. Waves wash over the dam, but they simply move underneath the trestle.

It is now next to impossible to cross the lake by train in daylight. The only two passenger trains cross at night, one eastbound, the other westbound. The freight trains don't take riders.

Another sad note was the dismantling of the original tracks around the northern end of the lake. Replaced by the trestle, this route was used occasionally to keep it operational, but in World War II the rails were ripped out for use in the war effort. The railroad bed remains and in places is used as a local road.

Several planes have crashed into the lake, some disintegrating as they hit the hard surface, some never found. The late Thomas C. Adams, commodore of the Great Salt Lake Yacht Club, told of participating in a dredging operation covering 125 square miles at the south end in search of a DC-3 owned by Standard Oil Company of California. It disappeared Saturday night, October 5, 1935. The three crewmen had asked Salt Lake Airport for landing instructions but never acknowledged receiving them.

After an extensive search, the body of one crewman was found, and the next day, a second. Efforts to locate the third body and the plane were unsuccessful, although two drifting seat cushions were found. Twenty-five feet beneath the surface, the plane was invisible; so a dredging operation was started that continued for several months. Searchers were determined to know the "why" of that crash. Not until the following year, nearly five months later, on February 27, was the plane hooked by a dragline halfway between the northern tips of Stansbury and Antelope islands. Cables were placed around the fuselage of the plane, and it was lifted a few feet off the lake bottom. Two boats took the cables, the submerged plane between them, and slowly moved twenty miles north to the Lucin Cutoff, where a crane would remove the plane from the water. If the boats moved more than two miles per hour, the plane would fly beneath the water, at one time striking the hull of one boat. At the trestle the plane was taken out, a two-day operation, dismantled, and shipped to California. Subsequent investigation concluded with the possibility that the plane crashed because of "a broken locking bar on top of one of the gasoline strainers which allowed air to enter gasoline lines and stop the flow of fuel to the engines."

The third crewman's body, dislodged from the wreckage by the dragline, was found two days after the plane was located. A Salt Lake City civil engineer, doing water development work in Tooele at the time, and his wife, recall vividly seeing the body. In a 1975 interview they said that even after five months in the water the man looked as if he had "died yesterday." Even the ring on his finger was intact — uncorroded. The brine, the cold of the winter months, and the absence of living things in the water had combined to preserve his body.

The lake still fascinates many people, but time has erased the mysteries and some of the original enthusiasm. It may take a future generation to discover the lake again, to know new and great resorts, and to hear the music of new bands.

Because of the lake's great fluctuations, its history of coming and leaving, of building and vacating, perhaps the businessman has grown tired of trying to outguess the fickle water level and refuses to believe that good times are ahead because the water is high again. But I believe that if we are to enjoy the lake, we must be as flexible as it is. My idea of a flexible resort is an artificial floating island in the middle of the lake, served by boats operating from a lake-penetrating pier, or even by hydroplanes skimming above the surface. Such a resort could operate right down to the final puddle of water.

Meanwhile, make your own best use of the lake and its many beautiful areas, depicted in this book.

The Southeast End

Home of the Great Salt Lake Yacht Club, the Silversands Marina is continually expanding for the great influx of sailors.

We now begin our tour around the lake. Its southeast end, where the Oquirrh Mountains slope into it — showing their spine later in the islands that extend to the Promontory Mountains — is the most familiar to tourists and native Utahns alike. Highway 80, a major transcontinental route, passes the shore here, the only area easily accessible from Salt Lake City. When the lake level is high, or even at medium level, the beaches are pleasant, the swimming excellent, and the view of the renowned sunsets unimpeded. Still, this is only a small part of the lake, showing practically nothing of the beauty and variety found elsewhere.

Of great interest in this sector is the budding Silver Sands Marina. Early in the morning — summer and winter — members of the Great Salt Lake Yacht Club can be seen rigging sails as they prepare for a race, a regatta, or a pleasure cruise. Sailors enjoy year-around activity since the water never freezes in the winter.

Because of the lake's rising level and its easy access, much attention is paid to the area, and almost daily plans for improving the lake are announced. After the state purchased the area in 1975, it annexed the beach front to the Great Salt Lake Park on Antelope Island.

Recreation-minded tourists and Utahns already are heavy users of the limited facilities — primitive showers and makeshift restrooms — on the southeast end. Eventually parking lots, a visitors' center, and changing-cabins will be built. The state has purchased the Silver Sands Marina, and efforts are being made not only to increase the number of docking stalls but also to improve all its facilities. In recent years the beaches have been sprayed against insects with some success.

Most of the celebrated resorts were situated in this area, and some of the skeletons remain. The foundation of Saltair is still visible in the distance off U.S. Highway 40 shortly after it makes the sharp turn from Salt Lake City. Some concrete foundations and the sand-filled pool make up the remainder of Black Rock Resort. Southward from this point, rows of gaunt pillars thrusting from the water in broken-tooth array are the remains of the Garfield pavilion.

Serving as a backdrop for this entire southeastern beach area is the Arthur Smelter of the Kennecott Copper Corporation, giving the visitor the feeling of being in some giant industrial complex. Though hardly an ideal scenic situation, the area is perennially popular because of its convenient location.

First-time visitors are surprised at the shallowness of the water and the distance they must wade in order to float. Many are content with wading. There are, however, two areas where deeper waters are close to shore, one directly west of Fritsch Island, the other around Black Rock.

Automobile drivers need to exercise care to remain on the roads and avoid the soft sands. Almost daily people become immobilized when they drive off the prescribed routes.

The freeway around the south end passes the Hardy Salt Company about four miles south of Black Rock. Several miles farther along, it passes through the southernmost tip of the lake when it is at high level. As the road curves westward, the traveler can see Stansbury Island in the distance to the right. At the south end of this island and the adjoining salt flats the American Salt Company has its solar plant. Some of the evaporation ponds and salt piles are visible from the highway.

Less than a hundred miles west from this point are the famous Bonneville Salt Flats where drivers have set automobile speed records. These flats were left over from the days when Lake Bonneville covered the entire

The concession stand at the Silversands Marina.

West from Fritsch Island toward Stansbury Island a calm and almost waveless lake belies its hidden fury and power.

Black Rock, almost surrounded by the lake with only a sand-filled swimming pool recalling the resort.

The Islander, *proud catamaran cruiser of the Silversands Marina, is a favorite attraction of the lake.*

Headquartering the marina office and a boat sales agency, this small building is also an outlet for cruise provisions.

The maiden voyage ended in disaster for this sailboat when the skipper lost control and crashed into the breakwater.

Straining hard, youthful beachcombers try to free their truck from the soft beach sand.

Interstate 80 to Nevada bisects the southern tip of the Great Salt Lake.

A meandering Jordan River winds its way across its delta toward distant Farmington Bay.

Sitting in the marshes of Farmington Bay, the buildings of a private hunting club reflect the early morning light.

area. It is possible to visit the race track, but during parts of the year it is covered with ground water. Those who have watched the races have at times seen strange mirages: racing cars apparently fifteen feet off the ground, people walking where there were no people, cities both rightside up and upside down, and inviting lakes where there was only dry desert land.

One area the tourist does not see so clearly as he travels toward Salt Lake City is that which is situated north and east of Saltair. As the road turns directly east toward the city (the Morton Salt Company is on the right), to the left are marshy areas fed by canals, creeks, and the Jordan River to the north. These marshes are the homes of many birds and several picturesque private duck and gun clubs. They can be seen best from the air since gates are locked against intruders.

Many of the channels and ponds are fresh water,

created by the meandering Jordan River. Because many birds nest here, a bird refuge was set aside near Farmington and was called the Farmington Bay Waterfowl Management Area. Part of it is accessible by automobile; so the visitor can observe the bird life. Even pelicans have found nesting grounds near Salt Lake City. An excellent though distant overview of these marshes can be obtained from Ensign Peak and other high elevations around Salt Lake City.

Sunsets in never-ending variety have awed people who watch from lookout points in the city or from the shore of the lake. Every evening, colors in the sky beam their reflections on the water. People who have seen this grandeur wait to drive on until the colors have faded. For many, the sunsets are the greatest attraction the lake has to offer. A sunset is a perfect ending to a visit at the southeast shore.

Antelope Island 5

Antelope Island, largest of the six major islands in the Great Salt Lake, is a little over fifteen miles long and about five miles across at its widest point. Frary Peak, highest of the island's mountains at 6,596 feet above sea level, shoulders 2,396 feet above the lake level when the surface is relatively high (at 4,200 feet above sea level). This rugged island, an exposed vertebra of the Oquirrh Mountains where this chain dips into the lake, is privately owned and used for livestock grazing except for the northern tip — the Great Salt Lake State Park.

No visitors are allowed on the private lands, but since this is the first comprehensive photo-book of the lake, I received the rare permission to land on the island with a helicopter in order to take pictures. The owner expressed the hope that visitors attracted by the hidden lands will not trespass but will travel on the island vicariously by viewing these pictures.

A firsthand look at the island can be obtained from boats along the western shores. Aided by binoculars, the sightseer can locate interesting landmarks, grazing cattle, and the rarely seen buffalo. The lake on this western side is quite deep, but the boater is advised to stay far enough from the shore to avoid sand banks and submerged rocks. Boating on the east side, through Farmington Bay, is not recommended, since the bay is shallow (three to four feet deep and less), and it is easy to get hopelessly stuck.

Captain John C. Fremont visited this island in 1845 and found antelope, some of which he and his men killed for food. In grateful recognition of this bounty, Fremont's party named the island for these graceful animals. Indians had reported that at one time buffalo were able to cross to the island on sandbanks but had disappeared when the lake rose. Captain Howard Stansbury likewise found antelope, along with other life, as he details in this excerpt from his 1850 survey report:

Saturday, June 15. Daylight found the boat at the mouth of the passage between Fremont and Antelope Islands, and, shortly after, we entered the beautiful little cove on the north-east side of the latter, from the banks of which several springs trickle down from the base of a small cliff of protruding rocks.

The scene was calm and lovely in the extreme. The rays of the rising sun, glancing brightly over the eastern mountains, shone upon the tiny ripples of the placid little bay, upon whose bosom a flock of snow-white gulls was calmly floating; while the green and gently sloping shores, covered with a luxuriant growth of rich and waving grass, contrasted strongly in our minds with the dreary and desolate waste of sand over which we had been roaming for the last month. Several little mocking-birds were singing gayly on the shore, and the shrill, cheerful whistle of the curlew resounded along the beach. Four graceful antelopes were quietly grazing on the grassy slope, while the cry of the wild duck, and the trumpet-note of the sand-hill crane were heard in the distance. The whole formed a picture which, in this desolate region, was as welcome as it was rare.

When the Mormons settled the valley of the Great Salt Lake, they changed the name of the island to Church Island, fittingly enough, since Brigham Young, leader of the Latter-day Saints Church, operated a herd of cattle on it. Brigham Young was fond of visiting the island; he used it for outings and enjoyed entertaining visitors on it. In 1850, three years after the Mormons arrived, Captain Howard Stansbury used the island as his base camp for his survey of the lake and its environs.

During the past hundred years or so, ownership as well as the type of livestock grazing on the island has

Rare find on a desert island: miner's lettuce.

Once travelled by thousands of visitors, the Antelope Island causeway awaits repairs after its washout.

West toward Stansbury Island a strange rock formation juts into the lake's water.

Spencer G. Lewis.

The author and a friend fight a stormy lake.

Spencer G. Lewis.

Elephant Head at the south border of White Rock Bay.

43

A piece of old mining gear on Antelope Island.

Range cattle seek out the shade of a leafless tree. Spencer G. Lewis.

Looking north along the shores of Antelope Island.

Wild buffalos and calves move up an island slope. Spencer G. Lew

Gerald Hatch.

Rendevous in White Rock Bay. Sailboats of the Great Salt Lake Yacht Club await evening for an overnighter.

A lonesome tree marks the site of the George Frary homestead and the unmarked grave of Mrs. Frary.

The Antelope Island ranch house.

Photographer Spencer Lewis is dwarfed by Split Pea Rock.

A birdseye view of the Antelope Island Ranch.

A buffalo herd flees from our approaching helicopter.

changed several times. Cattle, horses, buffalo, and sheep had their turns. Owners came and went, but none left as permanent a mark as the George Frary family, who came to the island in the early 1890s and operated a cattle ranch. Using a special cattle boat, Frary would transport up to forty animals to mainland markets. In his spare time he sailed the lake and soon was known as an authority on it.

After several happy years, the family idyll ended when Mrs. Frary had an appendicitis attack during a wild storm in 1897. George Frary spent the night fighting the waves on Farmington Bay in an effort to reach Salt Lake City for help. Exhausted, he arrived late the next morning, and after searching and pleading found a doctor willing to return with him. When they arrived later in the day, Mrs. Frary was dead. She was buried on the island. George Frary spent a total of about fifty years on and around the Great Salt Lake and helped take the soundings in 1902 when the Lucin Cutoff was to be constructed across the center of the lake.

In 1892 Frary used his cattleboat to haul twelve buffalo from Garfield Beach to the island for a permanent home. The herd grew to 400 head at one time; so some hunting was permitted to thin it out. The present small herd is the remnant of the original few.

Scenes for two motion pictures were filmed on the island. In 1922 the buffalo stampede scenes for the film *Covered Wagon* were shot there; in the late 1940s some of the exterior scenes for the film *The Sands of Iwo Jima* were shot.

More recently, an attempt was under way to make the entire island, as well as Fremont Island, a national park with a harbor, camping and picnic facilities, tennis courts, a shooting range, a museum, an eighteen-hole golf course, and a road running the length of the island to connect with the state park at the southeast shore. Pros and cons of the proposal were voiced in 1960, and the result was the establishment of a state park on the northern end with fewer facilities than had originally been planned.

A causeway was built to link the park with the mainland at Syracuse, but only a few years later rising waters washed out the road in places. The road has been repaired, and the park will reopen. It is to have a visitors center with concessions and facilities for picnicking, boating, and swimming. Some of the lake's finest beaches are on Antelope Island. And from several lookout points a traveler can enjoy spectacular panoramic views across the lake.

The causeway had an interesting side effect. When it cut Farmington Bay off from the rest of the lake, incoming fresh water pushed some of the salt water through the causeway opening. This made the bay into almost a fresh water lake which froze in the winter. Studies showed that the salt water would not mix readily with the fresh water, and although the top of the bay would freeze, a layer of salt water remained below.

In the warmer seasons, however, the fresh water was helpful to outboard motorists. After cruising on the Great Salt Lake, they would take a spin in Farmington Bay (close to the causeway where it is deep), then remove the boat from the water practically free of salt.

Two small islets, Egg Island and White Rocks, are adjacent to Antelope's northwestern shore, both heavily populated by nesting seagulls. Visitors have been asked to stay away from these rookeries, which are within the boundaries of the state park.

Scenic and fertile, Antelope Island is blessed with several fresh-water springs and a variety of vegetation. Besides the buffalo herd of about seventy head, it supports a large herd of cattle, and I have seen deer and coyotes on its slopes. Because of its scenic grandeur and its water supply, the entire island, according to some state officials, could be set aside for public use, with such facilities as horseback and hiking trails, good roads through scenic areas, and even hotels and luxury resorts.

The East Side

The gentle slopes and level plains skirting the east side of the Great Salt Lake are part of the Wasatch Front, so named because it borders on the towering Wasatch Mountain Range, part of the Rocky Mountains. From these mountains flow rivers and streams channeled into canals and ditches that irrigate the land, making it one of the fertile areas of Utah. Both outside and inside the cities and towns are hundreds of farms, pastures, orchards, and fields — rural Utah at its finest.

In the cities are great shopping centers, heavy industry complexes, factories, universities and colleges, and everything else needed to sustain the core of the state's population. Most tourists drive along the foothills and see the Great Salt Lake to the west — a perfect setting.

When the lake level is low, the fields border on miles of marshes and cracking mud flats. No one would think of walking across these to the inch-high water in the distance. The marshy flats are good for hunting, but many a hunter has had to pay for his bounty with a floundered car. A rising lake level, however, brings wonderful changes as the mud flats disappear and the lake often borders on green fields.

Several bird refuges are situated here near the lake; the largest and best-developed is the Bear River Migratory Bird Refuge, fifteen miles west of Brigham City. Sprawling across the delta of Bear River as it empties into the Great Salt Lake, the refuge encompasses 65,000 acres of marshes, mud flats, and open water. From the visitors center at the park headquarters motorists can drive around a twelve-mile loop on the dike of one of five artificial impoundments, getting close-ups of whistling swans, ring-necked pheasants, black-necked stilts, snowy egrets, herons, avocets, kildeer, phalaropes, and other species that walk and fly tamely among the cattails, salt grass, bullrushes, milkweed, tamarisk, and thistles. More than 200 species of birds can be seen at different times of the year. Fishing and hunting are permitted in some parts. A lookout tower is situated across from the visitors center.

Stansbury traveled through here in 1849 and was impressed by what he saw:

Moday, October 22 — Ther. at sunrise 25°. Morning clear and calm. The Salt Lake, which lay about half a mile to the eastward, was covered by immense flocks of wild geese and ducks, among which many swans were seen, being distinguishable by their size and the whiteness of their plumage. I had seen large flocks of these birds before, . . . but never did I behold anything like the immense numbers here congregated together. Thousands of acres, as far as the eye could reach, seemed literally covered with them, presenting a scene of busy, animated cheerfulness, in most graceful contrast with the dreary, silent solitude by which we were immediately surrounded.

Southeast of the refuge, about two miles west of Willard, Utah, is the well-developed Willard Bay State Park, a favorite recreation area in northern Utah. Here are facilities for camping, swimming, and fishing, a ramp for boat launching, and wharves. Here, for a few square miles, the Great Salt Lake has been turned into a fresh water lake, as the jumping fish attest.

From Syracuse a road leads west to connect with the causeway to the Great Salt Lake Park on Antelope Island. A drive through the rural communities near the lake can be enjoyable, but except for the causeway it is difficult to get to it conveniently from the east side.

The Lee Thurgood farm and West Point.

A look at the site of the old Bear River ferry.

The Bear River ferry near Corinne. (A Russell, 1869.)

From Weber Canyon toward the lake. (Russell, 1869.)

Same view as left, present day.

The launching ramp overlooking the fresh-water Willard Bay, an immediate neighbor of the Great Salt Lake.

Bear River near Corinne, as it meanders toward the marshes of the Great Salt Lake.

54

The railroad museum in Corinne.

View toward Antelope Island across Farmington Bay.

The American avocet, found at the Bear River Bay.

The Bear River Migratory Bird Refuge.

Fremont Island

Jutting hutlike from the brow of Fremont Island is Castle Rock, or Courthouse Rock, as authorized by Utah's Committee on Geographic Names, the island's highest peak at 4,995 feet above sea level, a bold crag that makes easy the identification of the third largest island in the lake. The peak, resembling a castle, is easily visible from the east bench and has become a well-known topographical mark. Rising abruptly from the six-by-two-mile island, the peak is 795 feet above the lake.

John C. Fremont was the first white man to visit the island when he and a small party of men rowed to it in an "India rubber" boat on Saturday, September 9, 1843, according to his journal. They had floated from the Weber River the day before, camped overnight at its mouth, then crossed to the island, hoping to find an exotic paradise. En route, the glued seams of the boat's air compartments started to come apart, and the men rowed frantically to reach the island, while one of them pumped the bellows to replenish the leaking air. Although happy to reach the island safely, their hopes of finding a fertile island were crushed when they saw bare rock slopes, dried grass, little shade, no trees or water or animals — a most inhospitable place. Fremont named it "Disappointment Island."

Ascending the summit, the men did enjoy a panoramic view of the lake and its surroundings. While Fremont did some sketching, the other men, including Kit Carson, chiseled a small cross into a rocky outcropping. The cross can still be seen.

Descending, the men decided to camp on the beach, where they enjoyed a rare treat — a night spent in absolute safety with no fear of Indians or other molestations. But they were awakened during the night by another type of annoyance — a loud pounding sound. Heavy winds had increased the surf, which was crashing into the shore and causing a slight trembling of the beach. As the wind worsened the next day, their return trip became a nightmare. At one point Fremont shouted to his men, "Pull for your lives! If we do not arrive on the shore before the storm commences, we will surely all perish!"

They arrived gratefully near Little Mountain and made it back to their base camp nine miles distant in time to avoid the downpour of a heavy thunderstorm. A howitzer was fired in joyful relief at the return of the

salty sailors. Their only loss was the brass cover to the object end of Fremont's telescope, left behind on the summit of the island.

The next visit of note was seven years later when Captain Howard Stansbury surveyed the lake. By this time the island had been renamed "Castle Island"; but Stansbury changed that, naming it after Fremont.

Stansbury noted his search for Fremont's lost lens cap, which he failed to find. His description of the island in the spring was favorable. He reported a luxuriant growth of grass and an abundance of sage reaching a height of eight feet and a stem thickness of up to eight inches. The men even saw a ground squirrel, although they were at a loss to explain where it obtained water. Blue herons had started laying eggs in the tall shore grass, and the man gathered some for food. They found a cross chiseled into a rock on the summit but were unable to explain its origin. (Fremont had neglected to mention this in his report, but it was identified later by Kit Carson.)

About ten years after Stansbury's visit, the island was used as a sheep range by Henry W., Jacob, and Dan Miller, giving way to the name, "Miller's Island," but ultimately the designation "Fremont Island" won out.

Wild and free, an island pony on the run.

During the occupation of the island by Miller's sheep, a most unusual guest was banished there. He was Jean Baptiste, a grave digger at the Salt Lake City cemetery, who, after the funeral parties departed and before he closed the grave, made it a habit to open the caskets just one more time and strip the corpse of any and all adornments. His ghoulish deeds were discovered after a body had to be exhumed for burial elsewhere and was found to be entirely naked, although the man had been dressed in a suit when interred. The subsequent investigation led to Baptiste's home where many boxes were found filled with burial gowns, shoes, and other items belonging to the dead. Some of the citizenry were so outraged that they probably would have killed Baptiste on sight had he not been carefully protected by the authorities. He was banished from humanity to Fremont Island. Henry and Dan Miller had a small cabin stocked with supplies on the island, and it was here that Baptiste was to spend the rest of his life. The Millers helped local authorities transport the man to the island; and when they returned to check up on him three weeks later, they found him safe and sound, having helped himself to the food. The next visit, three weeks later, presented a different picture. The cabin had been partially disassembled, probably to make a float with the wood, and Baptiste had escaped from the island. It has never been determined what became of him, although some people believe he may have drowned in the attempt. Almost thirty years later, in 1890, a skull was found in the Jordan River delta; and three years afterwards a partial skeleton was found, an iron ball chained to one leg. It was thought that this may have been the remains of Baptiste, although authorities denied that he had been shackled in any way. So the mystery has never been solved.

The Millers continued to raise sheep on the island, and one of them, Jacob, found the brass lens cover from Fremont's telescope.

In 1886, Probate Judge U. J. Wenner of Salt Lake City and his young family moved to the island and remained for the longest term of all. Judge Wenner had tuberculosis and had been ordered to live in the open air and in a dry climate. After building a small house of island stone, the Wenners spent five happy years on Fremont Island. They hired Charlie Rollins to herd a flock of sheep and obtained provisions monthly by boat, later

Fremont Island's east shore, south across Kit Carson Bay and Wenner Bay toward Antelope Island.

Keeping a lonely watch over Wenner Bay, Judge Wenner's home recalls idyllic days of a happy family.

Spencer G. Lewis.

Spencer G. Lewis.

Fremont Island, west shore view.

Fiery cacti blossoms on Fremont Island.

Spencer G. Lewis.

Spencer G. Lewis.

Fremont Island's rugged, wild, beautiful west shore.

The graves of Judge and Kate Wenner.

61

Kit Carson Rock.

Kit Carson's cross, about six to seven inches high.

The approximate area where Indian artifacts were found.

Cacti blossoms try hard to beautify a desert island.

View from Courthouse Rock east across the island and the Great Salt Lake toward the Wasatch Mountains.

Miller Point, the northwestern tip of Fremont Island.

obtaining their own boat, *The Argo.* Rollins became the runner between the island and civilization, returning with mail, food, and newspapers. The judge's wife, Kate, kept busy with household chores, teaching the children, and caring for her ailing husband. A small seepage of water, unobserved by Fremont and Stansbury, kept them supplied with fresh water.

Judge Wenner's sickness finally took its toll, and he died September 19, 1891, his last words reaffirming his love for Kate. They buried him on the island.

Although the family left Fremont Island after the burial, their life remained linked to it. Mrs. Wenner remarried, becoming Mrs. Kate Wenner Noble. When she died fifty-one years later, her daughter, Blanche, had her mother's ashes placed next to Judge Wenner's grave on the island. The graves and the ruins of their home are still visible.

The Wenners found arrowheads on the island, indicating an early Indian occupation. This is possible, since you can walk on dry land to the island when the lake is at 4,194.5 feet and lower.

Later, the Stoddard family of Hooper leased the island and discovered Indian artifacts which they made available for professional analysis. The samples, supposedly dating back 2,000 to 13,000 years, relate to no other Indian culture, making the Fremont Indians unique. Stone bowls, some unbroken, had been chipped completely out of rocks, placing the occupants in the preceramic periods of Utah. The Stoddards also found axlike weapons, some small round discs (some perforated with holes like buttons), hook and needlelike objects, and some objects of irregular shapes, the purpose for which is lost in time.

Another unique find was that of phallic symbols made of stone, something not found in any other culture in northern Utah. Bowls similar to those of the island are stone lamps made by the ancient Eskimos in Alaska, although a relationship between the two cultures cannot be assumed. All specimens had been picked from the ground, but a deeper exploration uncovered the remains of two skeletons, deteriorated so as to be useless for detailed evaluation. Dental fragments indicate that these two had been about six and eighteen years old.

In 1960 the island was purchased by the Richards family of Salt Lake City. It is now necessary to obtain permission to visit it. A wild herd of shetland ponies and a few unshorn sheep roam the island, grazing the slopes. Water is supplied by several drilled wells. An attempt was made in 1974 to round up the ponies, who were overgrazing the range; but they proved too cunning for their pursuers, and only a few were ferried to Promontory Point.

Ranchers on Promontory tell of a horse born on Fremont Island that was later removed. The horse was so homesick that it swam the three-mile channel, only to die on the island of suffocation because the salt had caked over its skin, eyes, and nostrils.

Although the Richards had purchased the island for recreational development, these plans have not been realized. The hope remains, however, for even though the island is bare, it has a magical quality; and those who have visited it have never lost the desire to return to it.

Fremont Indian bowls and a chipping tool.

The Promontory Area

8

Railroad history is linked to the Promontory Range, jutting into the Great Salt Lake from the north as the Promontory Peninsula. Some confusion has always existed concerning the names connected with the completion of the first transcontinental railroad. Many believe the historic line was completed at Promontory Point, but this is not true. Promontory Point is where the Promontory Range ends in the Great Salt Lake.

Others have called the place Promontory Summit, when, in fact, the town was situated in Promontory Hollow, slightly west of and below the summit. On today's maps this town is simply called Promontory, and although the old town is gone, it has been replaced by a visitors' center commemorating the completion of the first transcontinental railroad on May 10, 1869. Administered by the National Park Service as the Golden Spike National Historic Site, the area includes a section of rails on the original right-of-way and a fifteen-mile strip of the original railroad bed to be explored by the visitor. Replicas of the "Jupiter" and Union Pacific "119" engines face each other as they did at that May 10 celebration more than a century ago.

Although Promontory is off the main highway, that doesn't stop the visitors. They come by the hundreds as local people reenact the original ceremony every day during the summer. An especially grand celebration takes place every May 10, attended by local, state, and federal dignitaries.

A printed tour guide, available at the center, points out details to observe while traveling through mountain cuts and over grade fills. Still in evidence are the remains of parallel road beds, indicative of the competition between the rival railroads. Since no one knew where the companies would meet, they built past each other. Congress finally decreed the place, and parallel construction ceased on April 11, 1869.

Two miles southwest from the visitors' center at a low ridge, the lake becomes visible again some eleven miles distant across the Rozel Flats. Just beyond this ridge is a site marking the end of another railroading accomplishment, the laying of ten miles of track in one day by crewmen of the Central Pacific, a feat that has never again been equaled. A large sign marks the end of the tenth mile.

Privately owned, the Rozel Flats are used for livestock grazing, although a public road of dirt, rough in spots, slices southwest to Rozel Point. This is the location of a natural asphalt pit now inundated by rising water. The remains of buildings and abandoned equipment dot the area.

In the lake here the bather can be lifted high by the brine of the northern half of the lake, noticeably heavier than in the southern half. But swimming here is not too pleasant, as occasional strings of oil seep to the surface and cling to the body. They are hard to remove. Heavy oil deposits and floating debris from the decaying asphalt rigs line the shore, while large structures shrivel away in the water.

Climbing the mountain at this point and looking westward to the lakeshore below, you can see a unique sight — the Spiral Jetty. This is a work of art, bulldozed into the salt flats by the late Richard Smithson, who wanted to create art directly in nature. While he worked on it, the lake was low enough to expose sand banks next to the old shoreline, allowing Mr. Smithson to work on dry ground. Now the lake has covered the spiral he bulldozed into the sand, and the art work is best seen from a height.

On the east side of the Promontory Mountains a narrow blacktop road takes the traveler through East Promontory and past rustic farms to Promontory Point. The last ten miles of this thirty-mile stretch is a good dirt road. Since there are no commercial facilities along the highway, and since one has to return by way of the same road, it is important to have enough gasoline for the round trip. If the journey is measured from Corinne, the nearest town with gas stations, the trip to the Point and back totals 100 miles.

From the east side of the Promontory Mountains a magnificent panoramic view of the Wasatch Mountains across Bear River Bay can be seen. On Promontory Point one can see the railroad as it comes across Bear River Bay, skirts the Point, and heads out over the lake on the causeway. Directly south is Fremont Island, only three miles away across the Fremont Channel. The Lake Crystal Salt Company has an operation here, the salt settling ponds visible east of the road before it reaches the Point. Although the railroad tracks are fenced, it is possible to cross them at the salt plant and walk along the beach where Promontory Point ends and Great Salt Lake begins. Swimming here is pleasant, especially near the old loading ramp for Fremont Island-bound cattle,

A section of the wooden trestle of the Lucin Cutoff, still kept in good repair for use during storms.

A freight train heads west across the Lucin Cutoff. Empty freight cars in the water are used for shoring.

The driving of the golden spike à la 1973.

for the water is unusually clear, the beach is clean, and in places it has stepping stones into the deep water.

The road around the point to the west side of the mountain ends at a gate posted with "no trespassing" signs. Just around the corner is Little Valley, where rocks and sand were quarried to construct the Southern Pacific causeway.

Construction of this causeway, a mighty engineering job, was almost as great a feat as that of the transcontinental railroad. Following an extensive engineering study, a $49-million contract was awarded to Morrison-Knudsen, Inc., and from early 1956 to 1959 crews worked twenty-four hours a day seven days a week to complete the 12.6-mile causeway section.

First the lake bottom had to be stabilized to support the tremendous weight of the dam; so soft silt was dredged in channels up to forty feet deep, then replaced by sand and gravel. The foundation, depending on the type of lake bottom, ranged from 175 to 600 feet wide. For the causeway's construction, six bottom-dump barges hauling 2,000 cubic yards of sand and rock each trip were filled by conveyor belts and pushed to the dump site by 1,000-horsepower tugboats. With names like *Utah* and *Mayflower,* and complete with television, hot showers, and two-way radios, these tugboats became the Great Salt Lake Armada.

When a barge was in position to dump its load, the bottom would yawn open and the load would disappear into the lake in three seconds, causing an instantaneous eleven-foot change in the draft of the barge. To keep fill material coming, a total of 8¼ million pounds of explosives were used for eight near-Hiroshima-force explosions which crumbled the side of Little Valley Mountain. One of the eight blasts was the largest non-atomic explosion detonated up to that time. Two million one hundred thirty-eight thousand pounds of dynamite were set off to yield nearly eleven million cubic yards of rock fill.

When the causeway was almost to the lake's surface, flat-topped barges raised it above water level, bulldozers pushing rock and sand over the sides. A fleet of fifty trucks traveling from both sides of the lake hauled finishing material to raise the causeway twelve feet above the water. Fifty-three feet wide at the top, the causeway is wide enough for two sets of railroad tracks and a small service road. The bulk of the causeway is

Lake and land meet at the east shore of Spring Bay.

Looking north from the Rozel Hills to Coyote Point along the shore of the Great Salt Lake.

The Whitaker homestead near Bear River Bay.

Overlooking Promontory Point toward Fremont Island.

The Lake Crystal Salt Company's plant on Promontory Point.

The inundated Spiral Jetty *by the late Richard Smithson.*

Indian cave in the Promontory Mountains.

Sunset at Rozel Point, characterized by calmness, color, and deathly silence.

The actual landmark called Promontory Point. Here the Promontory Range meets the Great Salt Lake.

Eerie structures reach for life out of the rising waters of the lake at the Rozel asphalt pits near Rozel Point.

One of two culverts in the Lucin Cutoff, allowing for interchange between the northern and southern lake.

Pointing forlornly toward Fremont Island, a loading pier at Promontory Point awaits an occasional shipment of livestock.

never seen, since it lies below the surface. In cross section it is pyramidal, the bottom in places six times wider than the top and a maximum height, including material below the natural lake bottom, of ninety-seven feet. An estimated forty-three million cubic yards of material were moved to finish the job.

The capabilities of man during this project were awe inspiring. Morrison-Knudsen reported that during a single month 2,400,000 cubic yards of fill material were moved (105,000 cubic yards on peak days). Equipment used nearly ½ million gallons of diesel fuel in a month. The trench for the causeway foundation required the removal of fifteen million cubic yards of silt and clay.

To some of the construction men, the lake was just as awesome. When storms came up, the heavy brine packed a punch that caused cables more than two inches thick to snap, and sometimes heavy mooring cleats tore loose and sailed through the air like frisbees.

One night a runaway barge crashed into the old wooden trestle, knocked out some support pillars, and left the bare rails unbroken but suspended in midair. A flagman was summoned to stop the oncoming train. He arrived in a small motorized track car, failed to see the gaping hole, and dashed across the chasm, never leaving the tracks. He did not repeat this feat on the return trip.

Cutting across the lake directly west from Ogden, the new earth fill replaced the trestle section built in 1903, which had sliced forty-four miles off the old route. This saved seven hours, since the tortuous Promontory link was steep and curvy. The trestle across the lake, called the Lucin Cutoff after the town of Lucin where the old track met the new, had no grade, eliminating more than 1,500 feet of climbing on the old line, which had a grade as steep as ninety feet to the mile.

Division of the lake into northern and southern halves by the causeway resulted in some unexpected changes. It was believed that two fifteen-foot culverts would permit enough water interchange to keep the brine uniformly mixed. They did not. The southern half gets 95 percent of the fresh water inflow and is therefore being diluted, while the northern half builds up heavier salt content as the water evaporates.

Even so, exchange between the two divisions is taking place through the culverts in both directions simultaneously. As the lighter southern brine flows on top into the lower-leveled northern half, the heavy northern brine flows below through the culvert in the opposite direction. Even the causeway is permeable, and water from both halves flows through it. Dye tracers show a travel time ranging from nineteen minutes to several hours, depending on direction and place, but again, the interchange is not sufficient to cause an equilibrium. The dike has become a controversial subject, some people fearing that it might ruin the lake.

North from Little Valley along the west side of the Promontory Mountains are evidences that an Indian population resided here until the time of the white settlers. Of special interest are several caves used as shelters and a natural chute in the mountain through which the Indians chased buffalo. A steep drop-off at the end caused the animals to fall to their deaths, providing the tribesmen with easily obtained game.

These western areas are closed to visitors since all lands are privately owned and blocked by gates. The only way to see the area is from a boat on the lake or from a plane. Used chiefly for cattle and sheep grazing, the lands are similar to Promontory's east side but without a regular population.

An old ranch house gives welcome shade to local cattle.

The Northwest Area

9

Remote, dry, blazing hot in the summer, barren, and marked only by unimproved dirt roads, the vast area to the north and west of the lake offers few inducements to visitors. Yet there is in it one popular recreational spot — Locomotive Springs.

Some of these lands are used for grazing, especially in the winter, but during the summer as desert temperatures soar over the 100-degree mark, there is little activity. Little water flows in the northwest area; so it is important for the traveler to carry plenty. Except for the Kelton area there are no ranches or residents; therefore traveling is an adventure in which the motorist depends entirely on his own preparation and skill. No services are available anywhere until the traveler returns to Snowville, Tremonton, or Corinne or to Park Valley, a small ranch settlement with limited facilities.

Many things of interest are in the north and west areas but are so far removed from civilization that most people would hesitate to drive to them. Nonetheless, relatively safe to drive to, Locomotive Springs can be reached by a not-too-bad dirt road west from the Golden Spike historic site, or by a better but more circuitous route via Snowville and then by a twenty-mile good dirt road heading south to the lake.

The more interesting route is from the Golden Spike site from which the traveler crosses the North Promontory Mountains and the vast Salt Wells flats. Skirting the flats to the west are the Hansel Mountains, the tip of which ends in the lake at Monument Point. Here one can see the abandoned bed from the first transcontinental railroad. It is possible to drive on this bed back to the Golden Spike site, but some of the bridges are in poor condition and there are several detours.

It was at Monument Point that early parties moving West came through, including the Bartleson-Bidwell group, Bonneville's men, and Stansbury and his party. Lone Rock, the last rise of the Hansel Mountains as they end at the lake, was the scene of much activity as the railroad construction crews worked through the area. It was the backdrop of a historic photograph as the Jupiter engine pulled dignitaries from California to Promontory for the driving of the Golden Spike.

A few more miles west from Monument Point, around the southern slope of Indian Hill (an old Indian burial ground), are the Locomotive Springs, officially called Locomotive Springs Waterfowl Management Area. In the desert expanse these thermal fresh water ponds are a refreshing sight, where the traveler can see birds flying, fish jumping for insects, and green marshes lying beyond the ponds. The popularity of the springs is carried over into the winter months since the thermal properties keep the water from freezing, and fishing is possible at any time. The area is under the jurisdiction of the Utah State Department of Fish and Game, which administers it and stocks it with fish.

Approximately ten miles west of Locomotive Springs — reached by traveling the old railroad bed — is the town site of Kelton. Once a populous town with a school, the place is marked by the ruins of a few foundations, a fenced-in stagnant pond, and the deteriorated remains of a cemetery.

From Kelton the traveler can take a dirt road south along the northwestern side of the Great Salt Lake and the Hogup Mountains to a low rise at the south end of the mountains called the Fingerpoint. Other rough roads wind through the Hogup and Terrace mountains. Skirting the two mountain ranges on the west, the tourist reaches the Hogup Cave, a large cavern reportedly occupied by Indians for more than 8,000 years. Some excavating was done in the cave by the Department of Anthropology at the University of Utah, and more is planned; therefore, visitors are asked to refrain from disturbing the cave.

Civilization has had little effect on these dry mountains and deserts. Developments have always ended when water became scarce or too difficult to haul. Here a person can still experience what the pioneers saw before they began to colonize the land. And here he still gets that frightening feeling of being entirely dependent upon himself if something should go wrong with the car or if food or water should run out or if the heat should become overpowering. The north and west areas of the Great Salt Lake are those in which time is baked into immobility.

81

The Jupiter stops for a photograph with westbound wagon train, soon to be replaced by railroad service (May 1869).

A recent view of the site where the historic photo above was taken.

An abandoned Model A overlooks the vast Salt Desert from the slopes of the Terrace Mountains.

Dolphin Island and its shallow bay sit lonely at the northwest edge of the Great Salt Lake.

Hogup cave, occupied by Indians for over 8,000 years.

View of a thermal pond at Locomotive Springs.

The cemetery at Kelton.

Ancient Indian graves on Indian Hill.

85

A Hood's phlox, growing near the edge of a dirt road.

Globe mallow blossoms on Indian Hill.

86

Winter cattle at Monument Point. The view is across Spring Bay toward the Promontory Mountains.

Gunnison Island

10

The jewel of the northern Great Salt Lake and the only island of note in that sector is Gunnison Island. Only one mile long and a little over ½ a mile wide at its south end, with a total area of 155 acres, the island is made up of a small mountain ridge surrounded by five beautiful little bays. Rearing about 300 feet above the lake at the north end is the highest point, the Lion's Head, and the small island immediately north of this, called Cub Island. At lower lake levels the two are connected by a low ridge, forming a deep bay of striking beauty. Since the bay disappears and reappears according to the lake's level, I have named it Phantom Bay. At extremely high lake level, the two low hills making up Cub Island separate into two even smaller islets referred to as the Cubs — the Greater Cub and the Lesser Cub.

Heavy populations of seagulls and pelicans have been living on the island since long before the arrival of the white man. When Captain Howard Stansbury visited the island during his survey of 1850, he reported finding immense bird colonies:

Tuesday, May 7 . . .

The whole neck and the shores on both of the little bays were occupied by immense flocks of pelicans and gulls, disturbed now for the first time, probably, by the intrusion of man. They literally darkened the air as they rose upon the wing, and, hovering over our heads, caused the surrounding rocks to re-echo with their discordant screams. The ground was thickly strewn with their nests, of which there must have been some thousands. Numerous young, unfledged pelicans were found in the nests on the ground, and hundreds half-grown, huddled together in groups near the water, while the old ones retired to a long line of sand-beach on the southern side of the bay, where they stood drawn up, like Prussian soldiers, in ranks three or four deep, for hours together, apparently without motion.

Gunnison can be termed the most famous of the Great Salt Lake islands. Movie companies have filmed the pelicans, photographers and writers have publicized them, zoos have collected them, and a book was written about the island. In November 1895, Alfred Lambourne, a painter and author intrigued by Gunnison Island, decided to homestead on it and claim part of it for himself. He planned to grow grapes and subdue the dry soil. His experiences are described in his book,

Our Inland Sea, The Story of a Homestead.

A few months after his arrival, Lambourne had to share the island with a group of guano collectors who built a shack near his. One of the collectors unearthed a skull of an Indian underneath a ledge. Lambourne joined a further search:

A short distance from the spot where the skull was found, we exhumed more bones. There were a broken scapula, a clavicle, parts of a humurus, fragments of a spinal column, but no more. And, unlike the skull, these bones were in an advanced stage of decay.

Just below them we came upon the top of a slab that covered the tomb.

There, as it had reposed through the ages, was a skeleton complete. For an infinite time it must have lain in that narrow home. A weapon of stone — a huge, round battleax — lay by his side. Also there were many arrow-heads — of agate and jagged obsidian — also there were many round agates, which I supposed to be beads. Once the owner was a man of note.

During the time of Lambourne's occupation of the island, there were no pelicans nesting there. Evidently frequent visitors and guano collectors had frightened

A proud pelican mother shades her offspring from the sun.

89

Pelican males have a growth on their beaks. Here one displays it in proud profile.

While some pelicans guard their nests, others enjoy the beach and the air.

Spencer G. Lewis.

Gerald Hatch.

Young pelicans are tended in nurseries.

A pelican chick patiently awaits company.

Lambourne Bay, looking south.

A survey station, first erected by Stansbury's party, sits atop the Lion Head and marks the island's highest point.

Gunnison Island with Cub Island in the foreground, looking south across the lake.

them off. At the time, pelicans were nesting on Hat or Bird Island, a small islet north of Carrington Island.

For water, Lambourne was foresighted enough to bring with him a "small condensing apparatus," but water was also collected in rain barrels.

His vines did grow somewhat, but his success was limited because of the dry island ground.

Lambourne weathered fourteen months on the island and returned to civilization in February 1897. His homestead claim was never realized because of a competing mineral claim. Yet he did have a treasure. He had experienced the Great Salt Lake as no one else ever had. He came to know its moods from sunrise into the night, its weather from the calmest day to the fiercest storm, and its seasons from spring through winter.

Many years ago the pelicans returned to Gunnison, and there is a possibility that the island will be made into a bird refuge some day. Visitors are discouraged

from visiting the island since the nesting pelicans are very easily disturbed and may not return if they are interrupted too often.

Since Lambourne's occupation a few ornithologists have lived on the island for short periods to observe and study the bird life, but except for them and the return of the guano collectors and occasional visitors, the island has remained uninhabited.

About ten miles northwest of Gunnison Island lies Dolphin Island. Only seventy-five feet above the Lake and surrounded by vast salt flats, the island seems insignificant in comparison with Gunnison Island. It is about a mile long and a mile wide. Much of the time it is not even touched by the waters of the Lake, but at high lake levels a few inches of water fill a shallow bay on its south side. Dotted only by sagebrush, Dolphin is the only other island in the northern half of the Great Salt Lake.

Looking north from Cave Ridge toward the causeway with Gunnison Island in the distance.

11

Lakeside and Vicinity

On the west shore of the Great Salt Lake a short distance beyond the point at which the railroad causeway leaves the lake is a small railroad town, Lakeside, owned by the Southern Pacific Railroad. No services are available here, and most of the time a locked gate bars visitors. Consisting of a few trailers, some equipment and maintenance sheds, and a few parked railroad cars, the settlement has a population of railroad maintenance workers. They bulldoze riprap off nearby mountains, load it into dump cars, and place it along the causeway for reinforcement.

North of Lakeside is Strong's Knob, a 700-foot mountain standing lonely in the salt flats. When Stansbury and his party climbed it to place atop it a triangulation station, they discovered on its slope a large cave used by deer and antelope for shelter.

South of Lakeside are several mountain ridges and the Lakeside Mountains, rimmed along their western base by a good thirty-mile road from Lakeside to Interstate 80, making it possible to travel to Lakeside by automobile. When the road leaves Interstate 80, it parallels the main highway to the west, turns north, and for about fifteen miles is blacktopped, ending at the Hill Air Force Base extension. Just short of the base a dirt road forks from the blacktop and continues north for fifteen additional miles to Lakeside.

The first three miles of this road can be bad, since it cuts through a low-lying flat and after heavy rains may be under water. In the dry season, contrastingly, the road is of finest powder, spewing an awesome cloud of dust.

When he leaves the blacktop, the traveler enters a military reservation and is not permitted to deviate from the road until he exits from the reservation eleven miles farther north. Used as a bombing range, this area can be dangerous, since unexploded bombs may be lying about. At times, Air Force personnel will close the road to Lakeside until the bombing runs are completed and the roads checked.

Because the Intermountain Chemical Corporation has a solar evaporation complex near Lakeside and since the S.P. employees use the road frequently, the Lakeside residents are pushing to get the northerly fifteen miles blacktopped. Perhaps in a few years travelers can gain access to Lakeside on a surfaced highway.

Just south of the town, before the beginning of the Lakeside Mountains, are several low ridges extending from the northern tip of the Lakeside Mountains like the fingers of a hand. It is on one of these ridges, the Gillespies, where Aardvark Arch, never heretofore mapped or named, is situated. To reach the arch the traveler must take a rough jeep trail east across Death Ridge and Little Valley to Gillespie Pass along the border of the bombing range. The traveler must refrain from continuing south from the pass, or he will intrude on the bombing range. From Gillespie Pass, a short hike to the east slope of the Gillespies will bring Aardvark Arch into view.

Other ridges in the area contain caves, some of which had been homes for Indians. A few lived in the area when Stansbury came through, and after moving his survey camp from Strong's Knob he reported meeting a family of them — an aging Indian with his squaw and their child.

Wednesday, June 12.

. . . He was a Utah digger, and proved to be the same old fellow who had come to us last autumn, in Spring Valley, and who had engaged to bring in a "give-out" mule which we had left behind, for the promised reward

Aardvark Arch as seen from the shore of the lake.

The railroad town of Lakeside is occupied by railroad employees who work on the tracks and the causeway.

Most noted landmark south of Lakeside is Dearden's Knoll on the Hill Air Force Base bombing range.

of a new blanket. I questioned him about the mule, but he only laughed and would give me no satisfaction. The poor donkey had doubtless furnished his lodge with meat for the winter. He was an old man, nearly sixty, quite naked, except an old breech-cloth and a tattered pair of moccasins. His wife was in the same condition precisely, minus the moccasins, with a small buckskin strap over her shoulders in the form of a loop, in which, with its little arms clasped around its mother's neck, sat a female child, four or five years old, without any clothing whatever. She was a fine-looking, intelligent little thing, and as plump as a partridge. The mother seemed to evince much affection for it, and was very much pleased when I threw over its shoulders an old piece of scarlet flannel which had been torn from one of the stations by the wind. I noticed, however, that after they left us, and she thought herself out of our sight, the cloth was fluttering from her own person, and the baby was as destitute as ever. I gave them something to eat, and, what I suspect was more welcome, a hearty draught of water. The poor child was almost famished. The old man was armed with a bow and a few arrows, with which he was hunting for ground-squirrels.

Even though a large part of the area south of Lakeside cannot be explored because of the bombing range, a three-mile section of lakeshore directly south of the causeway can be. From several high peaks west of the dirt road and immediately south from Lakeside — Twin Hills (elevation 4,982 feet) — you can obtain a panoramic view into the bombing range and surrounding areas.

Along the south end of the Lakeside Mountains on their west side is a large quarry and on the east side is the Rowley Plant, an operation engaged in extracting magnesium from the waters of the Great Salt Lake.

An abandoned pickup truck awaits final disintegration on the slopes of Death Ridge, south of Lakeside.

Carrington Island

12

Bleak, desolate, and difficult to approach, Carrington Island, 1½ miles square and 527 feet above the water, is the fourth largest island in the Great Salt Lake. From its highest point, Lambourne Rock, gentle slopes descend to the shore where rocky beaches meet the water. Devoid of fresh water, the island's growing season depends upon winter and spring moisture falling on the slopes. Boulders dot the landscape, and the June grass, green for only a short time, turns brown to complement the color of the rocks.

To the west, large sand banks and mud flats skirt the island, making impossible rounding it by boat.

Stansbury visited the island twice, and his description of it is still applicable after a century and a quarter:

Tuesday, April 9. The island was between six and seven hundred feet high, and six and a-half miles in circumference. As we ascended the slope of the hill, which is much more gentle than that of any other island in the lake, small rolled stones, sand, and gravel are first met with, then slate, covering the ground in broken lamine; and the summit consisted of ledges of excellent roofing slate, of which any quantity can be obtained. The latter was filled in places with cubes of bisulphuret of iron, which frequently penetrated several laminae. I searched diligently, but could find no cubes free, although the rock was full of the small cavities from which they had either been dislodged or had decayed under the influence of the weather. Abundance of the slate can be procured free from this objection; and by trial I ascertained that a nail could be driven through the layers almost as easily as through a shingle. On the shores were large quantities of a deposite resembling hard clay, which had formed when soft upon the rolled stones of the beach, and, when hardened by the sun or other causes, had been broken off, retaining, like a hollow mould, the shape of the stone upon which it had been deposited. The island is surrounded by extensive shoals. The beach is gradually making to the south, and will doubtless join with the wide sand-flats to the south and west before many years.

Interestingly, Stansbury was unable to find any loose cubes of bisulphuret of iron, even though he could see the cavities from which they had fallen, as well as other cubes held in the rocks. These cubes are also found in some rocks on Fremont Island and are so interesting as to be picked up by everyone seeing them. It is possible

that Indians, who had access to Carrington Island at the time, picked them up to use as playthings.

After the surveyors left, no one seems to have had any use for the island. It remained unused and unoccupied until another lake explorer, Charles Stoddard, homesteaded there in 1932 with the idea of using it as a sheep ranch. He built a log cabin and moved in with his wife and three children. But he was never able to get enough fresh water, and with the added menace of marauding coyotes traversing the sand banks connecting the island with the mainland, he was forced to give up the venture. Later, he started a sheep ranch on Fremont Island.

During World War II, the Strategic Air Command used Carrington as a practice target. Flying nonstop from as far away as Texas, bombers would hit the target day and night, and by the war's end Carrington had taken a beating as severe as that of any European city.

In 1960 the island was turned over to the Bureau of Land Management.

Less than four miles north of Carrington Island is a small islet called Hat Island, also known as Bird Island, inhabited by various kinds of birds. Only seventy-five feet high, and a little over ½ mile in circumference, the islet is of conglomerate rock with sparse vegetation. When the surveyors visited the island in 1850, no birds nested on it, and only a few nest on it now. But around the turn of the century pelicans and commerants nested here by the thousands. The spectacle was such that a landing ramp was built for boats, and excursions were conducted to the island. Because of this intrusion of man and a subsequent drop of the lake level, the island became unsafe for the birds. Coyotes could walk dry-pawed to the island on sand banks and salt flats and help themselves to the young birds. So the pelicans returned to Gunnison Island.

One other island lies in the vicinity of Carrington — Badger Island. It is mentioned only for the sake of completeness since it does show up on some lake maps. Badger Island lies four miles south of Carrington and is hardly worthy to be called a sandbar, with its five-foot elevation and sparse sagebrush growths. It disappears under water when the lake rises to the 4,205-feet level. Someone with a good sense of humor must have named it during a moment of frivolity. This is one "island" in the lake you can skip.

103

Great boulders dot the northeast slope of Carrington Island.

Reminiscent of Easter Island, a great natural stone head overlooks the slopes of Carrington.

Gerald Hatch.

World War II bombing scars on Carrington Island.

Gerald Hatch.

Carrington Island, looking south toward Stansbury Island.

105

Gerald Hatch.

Shore section of Bird Island.

Gerald Hatch.

View from Carrington Island to tiny Bird (or Hat) Island.

The rusty shell of a bomb brings back memories of a time when the island was off limits to visitors.

Bird, or Hat, Island is an occasional nesting site.

The final stop in our armchair circumnavigation of the lake is Stansbury Island, second largest in the chain. This is my favorite island. Captain Stansbury, too, felt that this island was the most hospitable of all, superior even to Antelope Island. And I'm sure his sentiment did not stem alone from the fact that the officers in his party named it after him. This was the third island named after men in the survey crew, the others named for Lieutenant J. W. Gunnison, who had accompanied the survey party from the East, and Albert Carrington, a resident of Salt Lake City, hired to assist in the survey.

Reliable fresh water springs on the east side of the island and producing wells on the west side make this an excellent range for cattle. A rich juniper growth, casting pleasing dark spots against even the highest ridges, give the hiker welcome shade. Bold cliffs and rock formations, sandy beaches and bays, majestic peaks, and nestled valleys combine to make this island a rugged paradise. From lofty heights you can view spectacular panoramas across the Great Salt Lake, and in the evening red and golden hues across cliff and pinnacle paint a picture impossible to duplicate with brush or lens.

Sunny and calm or cloudy and stormy, the lake at Stansbury becomes a vivid experience. One of my favorite places is Sandy Beach Bay, just below the northernmost tip of the island on the east side. Although it is shadeless, with a beach umbrella I consider this bay my secret South Pacific island. After Stansbury's crew had erected a triangulation station on the first hill of the island, they ". . . encamped upon the white-sand beach of a lovely little bay [Sandy Beach Bay] indenting its eastern shore."

Running the length of the island on the west side is a good improved dirt road, easily reached via Interstate 80 by taking the Stansbury exit west of Grantsville. After the road leaves the freeway, it extends sixteen miles across salt flats and evaporation ponds, then along the island, ending at the west tip of Crystal Bay. At this point a locked gate prevents visitors from continuing onto a private dike that impounds ponds operated by the National Lead Company's Magnesium Division.

Just short of the end of the road at the locked gate a small and totally unimproved jeep trail climbs a low ridge and eventually rims Crystal Bay. On the east side of the bay it climbs a steep ridge into Sandy Beach Bay.

The traveler should tackle this road only with a four-wheel drive vehicle, preferably equipped with a winch, or should have enough people to help push it past two tricky sand traps.

The visitor encounters the first trap shortly after he leaves the main dirt road as the trail to Sandy Beach makes a ninety-degree turn to parallel Crystal Bay, the second about 6/10 of a mile farther where the trail makes another turn. It is advisable to clear any obstructions from the traps before driving through. The driver should enter the trap with a momentum powerful enough to carry the vehicle through, but in a gear low enough to make shifting unnecessary. If you shift in a sand trap the wheels halt, momentum is gone, the wheels dig straight down into the sand, and the vehicle is stuck.

Use care in negotiating the last steep ridge into Sandy Beach Bay since the hillside is strewn with rocks that could damage the underside of a vehicle. The return trip presents another problem. Since the ridge is steep, you should make certain the vehicle can climb back out before you go in. At the end of the road at the bay you should refrain from going off the grassy areas; the soft beach sand does not support the weight of a vehicle.

After the second sand trap, another jeep trail takes off southeasterly, climbing another high ridge. From here the Great Salt Lake can be seen again. Although the trail continues down the other side high above the lake, I do not recommend that even jeeps continue south. The trail becomes so rocky that even high-clearance vehicles can't make it without damaging their undersides.

To avoid entirely the problem of getting stuck, I simply park my car on the main dirt road and hike to Sandy Beach Bay, a distance of 1 1/3 miles. Alternatives to this are going in by motorcycle or dune buggy.

The entire northern tip of the island is small enough to make enjoyable exploration by foot. The drive or hike to Sandy Beach Bay is always an exhilarating experience. As you climb the last ridge before reaching the shimmering bay, the entire lake presents itself in a cinemascopic panorama. The view stretches from beyond Promontory Point through Brigham City and Ogden, along the Wasatch Front and Antelope to Salt Lake City. From higher elevations you view an even wider scene.

From high atop the island, a spectacular view unfolds across the lake toward Antelope Island.

Stansbury Island's Boulder Point, with Sandy Beach Bay on the left and Crystal Bay on the right.

Great Boulders litter a steep slope on Stansbury's west side.

Winter view of the island's highest point, the Dome.

Dead juniper branches, frozen in their last plea for moisture.

Blossoms of a cactus pod bring color and cheer to a desert island.

Looking southeast along Stansbury's shore and beaches toward the Oquirrh Mountains.

High surf rolls into Sandy Beach Bay. Surf forms only on stormy days.

View looking north across Stansbury Island.

Sandy Beach Bay.

The American Salt Company's Solar Division at the south end of Stansbury Island with evaporation ponds in the distance

Clear and deep, the water at the bay is the finest in the lake for swimming. Incoming waves splash upon magnificent boulders bordering a white, sandy beach. On windless days the bay lies mirror-calm, a perfect place to float.

The hiker may also experience the zest of exploration by climbing the three last hills of the island as they thrust into the deep waters at Boulder Point and higher reaches along the island's center ridge, such as Adams Peak (elevation 6,061 feet) or the Dome — highest point on the island (elevation 6,609 feet — more than 2,400 feet above the lake). On the slopes of the west side are a short mine shaft and some small caves. Wide ledges have been cut into the mountainside by the waves of Lake Bonneville. Huge conglomerate stone masses rim some mountains halfway up the slopes, formed and pressed together by the waves of ancient times as they slashed at the shore.

The entire island, eleven miles long and three miles wide, is used for grazing, and part of it is privately owned. Some "no trespassing" signs have been posted, but the beaches as well as other areas are Bureau of Land Management-administered lands to which the public has legal access. To retain this right and to preserve the area for future enjoyment, today's user must, of course, help prevent fires and other erosion-causing activities.

Since the main dirt road along the west slopes dead-ends, the visitor must double back on it as he returns to the freeway. On this freeway from the island to Salt Lake City, he will cross the northern end of Tooele Valley, a beautiful gently sloping bowl sheltered on three sides by mountains. These are the Stansbury Mountains on the west, the Oquirrh Mountains on the east, and a low mountain ridge on the south. A large section of the Stansbury Mountains is part of the Wasatch National Forest and has picnic and camping facilities, mountain trails, and icy streams and lakes. This is a high mountain paradise, cool and refreshing on the hottest summer day — in the middle of a desert.

Equally refreshing are the Oquirrh Mountains with their cool and shady canyons and windy peaks. The range can be crossed on a steep and circuitous dirt road from Tooele into the Salt Lake Valley. The ride is adventurous, the sights magnificent, and the extra travel time worth it. From Tooele the road leads through Middle Canyon to the summit and descends on a Road-to-Burma type of mountain cut into the Salt Lake Valley by way of Butterfield Canyon. On the summit another road winds even higher to a spectacular lookout point behind and above the great open copper pit of the Kennecott Copper Company.

From the peaks of the Oquirrh Mountains you view a stunning panoramic view not only of the valleys below but also of distant mountains. You can see the Great Salt Lake, deserts and mountains north into Idaho, and Utah Lake and the mountains beyond it to the south — all from one point.

At this point we have gone full circle around the lake — one of the marvels of the world — and we have a last chance to see the lake and to reflect. What will become of it? How long will the present rising cycle last? Will it shrink even more the next time it recedes? Will it ever disappear completely, or will some future ice age bring back a fresh-water Lake Bonneville?

The answers lie in the future, but today the lake serves salty sailors, frolicking bathers, and children who don't have to know how to swim; they can float.

The small hamlet called Great Salt Lake City is gone.
But the mountains have remained, though quarry-scarred —
   Silent, stone-faced witnesses.
And the Great Salt Lake
   Still sparkles in the rising morning sun.

A panoramic view looking north across the island with the Promontory Mountains in the distance.

Bibliography

Adams, Thomas C. "Searches for Lost Aeroplanes in the Great Salt Lake." Unpublished ms, pp. 1–12.

American Guide Series. *Utah, a Guide to the State.* Compiled by the Works Progress Administration. New York: Hastings House, 1940.

Bolton, Herbert E. *Pageant in the Wilderness.* Salt Lake City: Utah State Historical Society, 1972.

Hearings Before the Subcommittee on Public Lands of the Committee on Interior and Insular Affairs, United States Senate, Eighty-sixth Congress, Washington, D.C., U.S. Government Printing Office, 1: 1–180. Salt Lake City, November 10, 1960; Ogden, Utah, November 12, 1960.

Kraus, George. *High Road to Promontory.* Palo Alto, California: American West Publishing Company, 1969.

Lambourne, Alfred. *Pictures of an Inland Sea.* Salt Lake City: The Deseret News Press, 1902.

Lambourne, Alfred. *Our Inland Sea, the Story of a Homestead.* Salt Lake City: The Deseret News Press, 1909.

Madison, R. J. "Effects of a Causeway on the Chemistry of the Brine in Great Salt Lake, Utah." *Water Resources Bulletin.* Utah Geological and Mineralogical Survey 14 (1970): 1–52.

Miller, David E. *Great Salt Lake Past and Present*, 2d ed., rev. Salt Lake City: Utah History Atlas, 1969.

Morgan, Dale E. *The Great Salt Lake, 1947.* Reprint. Albuquerque: University of New Mexico Press, 1973.

Morrison Knudsen Company, "Salt Lake Causeway Nears Finish." *Em-Kayan* 18 (1959):6–8.

Nielsen, Vaughn S. *Golden Spike Tour Guide.* Globe, Arizona: Southwest Parks and Monuments Assoc., 1975, pp. 1–20.

Price, Raye Carleson. *Barrier of Salt, the Story of Great Salt Lake.* Salt Lake City: Deseret Book Co., 1970.

Rudy, Jack R., and Stoddard, Earl. "Site on Fremont Island in Great Salt Lake." *American Antiquity* 25 (1960):285–90.

Stansbury, Howard. *Exploration and Survey of the Great Salt Lake Valley, Utah.* Philadelphia: Lippincott, Grambo & Co. 1 (1852):87–110.

United States Department of the Interior. "Bear River Migratory Bird Refuge." 1–20, 1968.

Zimmerman, Leonard F. "Will the Great Salt Lake Rise Again?" *Morton Spout.* January 1957, pp. 16–20.

About the Author

PETER G. CZERNY was born in Guben, Germany, in 1941 and remembers many harrowing experiences that occurred during and after World War II. He, with four other children and his parents, lived in East Germany (officially called the German Democratic Republic), from which they escaped in 1952. After 1½ years in refugee camps in West Germany, they emigrated to the United States.

As a child in Germany, Peter was intrigued when he read about a great salt lake in America, where people could sit upright in the water and could float without having to know how to swim. He yearned to visit the lake one day. When they arrived in the United States and through a fortunate set of circumstances, his family located near the lake, and his interest in it developed into an absorption that has never waned. We are the beneficiaries of his absorbing interest in the Great Salt Lake as we read of his experiences and see through his camera's eyes the places he has officially named.

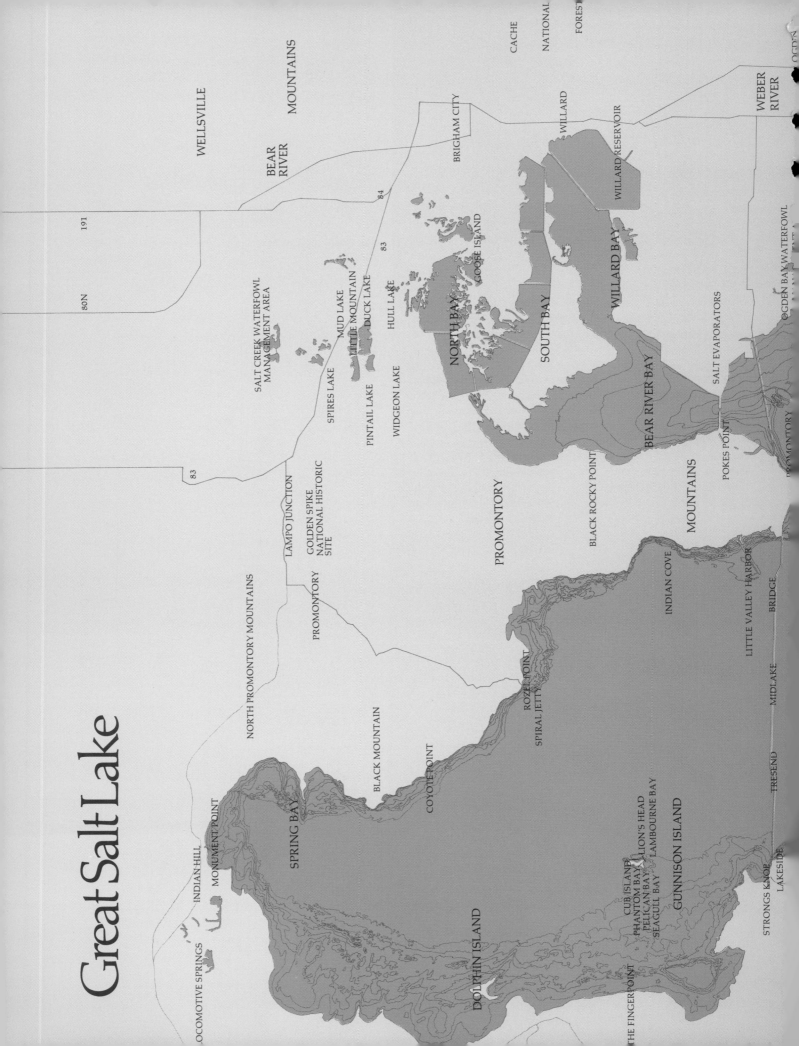

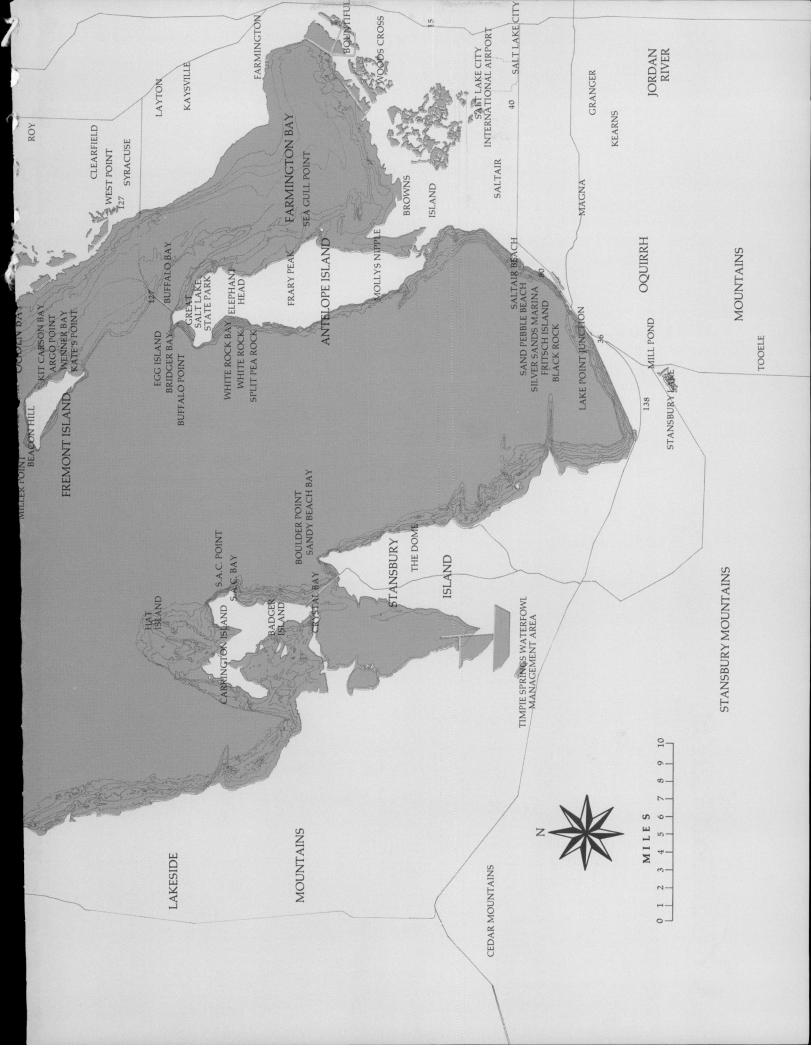